INVESTING WITHOUT THE NOISE

Unlocking the Powerful 9-Factor Investment Model

Kunal Khatri

Synopsis
Investing Without the Noise

Cut through the clutter. Invest with clarity.

In a world flooded with opinions, headlines, and hype, *Investing Without the Noise* offers a refreshing, simplified path to financial wisdom. Whether you're a seasoned investor or just beginning your journey, this book is your roadmap to making smart, informed, and emotion-free financial decisions.

Written by seasoned advisor Kunal Khatri, this book unpacks the essentials of investing—without the jargon or overwhelm. From understanding asset classes and risk to mastering the art of asset allocation, compounding, and behavior-driven decisions, every chapter is designed to empower you with practical insights that work in real life.

Kunal introduces his transformative **9-Factor Investment Model,** a crystal-clear framework that demystifies the most important questions every investor faces: Where to invest? What returns to expect? How to navigate risks? And perhaps most critically—**how to**

manage your own behaviour when markets turn volatile.

This is not just another book about numbers—it's about mind-set, discipline, and purpose-driven investing. Learn how to align your investments with your life goals, avoid costly emotional pitfalls, and use timeless principles like rupee cost averaging and the power of compounding to your advantage.

At its core, ***Investing Without The Noise*** is a guide to mastering **behavioural alpha**—the edge that truly sets successful investors apart in today's data-drenched world.

Insightful. Grounded. Actionable. This book will help you tune out the chaos and tune in to what truly matters—**building wealth with wisdom, patience, and purpose.**

Contents

Foreword

The word "Investing" holds a unique fascination. It sparks curiosity and excitement, urging us to dive into the world of financial growth. In the Indian context, this fascination is heightened because, surprisingly, investing and money management aren't widely taught in schools. We are rarely educated about the importance of saving, managing money, or making disciplined financial decisions. As a result, most of us only start engaging with money management when we begin earning.

Additionally, the financial world is full of noise and overwhelming choices, with new data circulating every day. This often leads to the belief that financial literacy is low, managing money is difficult, and investing is an intimidating task. And, of course, the idea of making more money always piques our interest.

While these challenges may explain why many of us are not well-versed in personal finance, the good news is that it's never too late to learn. In this book, I aim to break down various aspects of money, investment decision-making, and the process behind it, so you can approach investing with confidence.

What is Investment?

At its core, investing is the act of acquiring an asset with the goal of generating income or appreciation, or both. Let's break this down:

1. **An Asset** - something of value.

2. **Acquired with a Goal** - a clear objective behind the investment.

3. **To Generate Income** - a source of earnings.

4. **To Get Appreciation** - growth in value over time.

This simple definition opens the door to deeper understanding, and it's equally important to comprehend the decision-making process behind investments.

In my experience as an investment advisor, I have found that people often ask two questions when it comes to investing: "Where should I invest?" and "What return can I expect?" But the reality is, investing involves much more. There are several other key questions we need to answer to make informed decisions:

1. Where should we invest?

2. What return can we expect?

3. What is the cost of investment?

4. What risks are involved?

5. How easily can we acquire the investment?

6. How easy is it to exit from the investment?

7. How should we behave with our investments?

8. Why are we investing in the first place?

9. How do the market and economy affect our investment?

By addressing these nine crucial questions, we can make informed and appropriate investment decisions.

Why I Wrote This Book

Investing is not just about deploying money; it's about making our hard-earned money work for us. It's a process that blends mathematics, emotions, goals, and behaviour to make decisions that favour our financial future. If we fail to answer the essential questions or neglect the right approach, we risk making poor investment choices that could hinder our progress.

This book introduces a nine-factor model to help you make sound investment decisions, focusing not only on the technicalities but also on the human behaviours that impact our choices. While there are many books on investing, my goal here is to simplify the key factors that lay the foundation for successful investing, making it more accessible for everyone.

I have distilled all my knowledge on investment decision-making into this book, and I believe it will guide you in defining the scope of your own investment journey. I hope this book serves as a valuable tool in helping you achieve the ultimate goal of financial freedom.

Chapter 1

Return on Investment (ROI)

Understanding the Key to Smart Investing

When we embark on our investment journey, the first step is simple: save money, choose an asset, and invest. But there's one important question we need to answer before making any investment decisions: **Why are we investing?**

At its core, investing means putting money into something with the expectation of earning a return. This return is what we call **Return on Investment (ROI).** But what exactly is ROI, and how do we calculate it?

What is ROI?

Let's say you invest Rs. 1 lakh, and you make a profit of Rs. 10,000. The return on your investment (ROI) would be Rs. 10,000, and in percentage terms, your ROI would be 10% (calculated as Rs. 10,000 ÷ Rs. 1,00,000 * 100).

So, the basic objective of investing is clear: to earn a profit or income.

How Does ROI Work?

ROI can come in two main forms:

1. **Regular Cash Flows**: Earnings from investments, like dividends, interest, or rent.

2. **Capital Appreciation:** Growth in the value of the investment itself, such as an increase in the market value of stocks, real estate, or art.

The formula for ROI combines both these factors:

ROI = Growth Yield + Earnings Yield

Here's a simple example:

Investment	Cash Flow	Capital Appreciation	Earnings Yield (%)	Growth Yield (%)	ROI (%)
1,00,000	5,000	5,000	5%	5%	10%

Thus, ROI is a measure of how effectively your investments are performing. It tells you if the money you invested is bringing in returns.

But Is ROI Really the Whole Picture?

Not exactly! ROI doesn't capture the costs involved in making an investment. Just like there's no such thing as a free lunch, there's no gain without some cost. When you invest in something, you expect a profit, but there are expenses that come with it.

There are two types of costs to consider:

1. Actual Cost

This is the real, out-of-pocket money you spend to acquire, carry, and eventually sell an asset. This includes costs like:

- Purchase price of the asset

- Maintenance or carrying costs

- Taxes and duties related to the asset

2. Notional Cost

Unlike actual costs, notional costs don't require a direct cash outflow. However, they still impact your ROI. These costs are "imaginary" in the sense that they represent missed opportunities or other conceptual losses, like the **Time Value of Money**.

The Impact of Time: Time Value of Money

As the saying goes, **"Time is money."** The value of your money doesn't stay constant over time. Inflation, a key notional cost, eat away the purchasing power of your money. If you don't invest or use your money wisely today, it will lose value tomorrow.

Example: Let's say an item costs Rs. 100 today, and the inflation rate is 10%. In a year, that same item will cost Rs. 110. This means the value of your money decreases over time due to inflation.

This concept is called **Purchasing Power Parity**—and it's important to consider, because if you don't factor in inflation, the real value of your returns will be less than expected.

Real ROI: The Inflation-Adjusted Return

To understand the true value of your investment, we need to account for **inflation**. By subtracting the impact of inflation from your ROI, you get the **Real ROI**, which reflects the true, inflation-adjusted returns on your investment.

Why Is Real ROI Important?

Real ROI helps you conclude whether your investment is beating inflation. It allows you to assess which assets are truly generating value after accounting for the eroding effects of inflation. By understanding real ROI, you can compare different asset classes to identify the ones that offer the best inflation-adjusted returns.

In conclusion, understanding ROI isn't just about knowing how much you earn, but also about accounting for costs—both actual and notional—and inflation. By doing so, you ensure that your investments are truly growing and protecting your wealth in the long run.

10-Point Summary of ROI: Understanding the Key to Smart Investing

1. **Definition of ROI** – Return on Investment (ROI) measures the profitability of an investment, calculated as (Profit ÷ Initial Investment) × 100.

2. **Types of ROI** – ROI can come from **regular cash flows** (like dividends, interest, or rent) and **capital appreciation** (increase in asset value).

3. **ROI Formula** – ROI = **Growth Yield + Earnings Yield**, where Growth Yield represents capital appreciation and Earnings Yield represents income from the asset.

4. **Limitations of ROI** – ROI does not account for the costs associated with making an investment, which can reduce actual profits.

5. **Types of Investment Costs** – Costs include:

   o **Actual Costs** – Direct expenses like purchase price, maintenance, and taxes.

   o **Notional Costs** – Indirect costs like the opportunity cost of capital and time value of money.

6. **Time Value of Money** – The value of money decreases over time due to inflation, impacting the real worth of investment returns.

7. **Inflation's Effect on ROI** – Inflation erodes purchasing power, meaning a nominal return might not reflect true gains.

8. **Real ROI (Inflation-Adjusted ROI)** – By subtracting inflation from ROI, investors get a clearer picture of their actual returns.

9. **Importance of Real ROI** – Helps investors determine if their investments are truly growing in value after considering inflation.

10. **Smart Investing Strategy** – A good investment is one that generates a **positive real ROI,** covering both costs and inflation, ensuring long-term wealth growth.

Chapter: 2

Where to Invest?: Understanding Asset Classes and Their Performance

Now that you have understood the concept of Return on Investment (ROI), the next logical step is to decide where to invest. Making the right investment decision requires a clear understanding of different asset classes, their characteristics, performance, and the risks involved. This chapter will help you explore the classification of assets and guide you in selecting the appropriate asset class for investment.

Classification of Assets

For investment purposes, assets can be broadly classified into two categories:

1. **Physical Assets**

2. **Financial Assets**

Each of these categories has unique characteristics, advantages, and risks. Let's dive deeper into their details.

1. Physical Assets

Physical assets are those assets which one can touch & feel, having a real existence and are used by individuals or institutions to generate value. These assets usually require maintenance and can sometimes be illiquid, meaning they may not be easy to sell quickly. However, they provide stability and can act as a hedge against inflation.

Examples of Physical Assets:

- **Real Estate**: This includes commercial properties, residential buildings, land plots, and other real estate investments. The value of real estate generally appreciates over time, making it a preferred investment option for long-term wealth accumulation.

- **Commodities**: Gold, silver, copper, crude oil, and other natural resources fall under this category. Many investors use commodities as a hedge against inflation since their prices tend to rise when the cost of living increases.

- **Art & Collectibles**: Sculptures, paintings, antique pieces, and other unique artifacts are also considered physical assets. Their value depends on rarity, demand, and artistic significance.

- **Vehicles (Vintage Cars & Collectibles)**: Classic and vintage cars, as well as limited-edition vehicles, can be valuable investments. They often appreciate in value based on demand, condition, and historical significance.

Performance of Physical Assets

- **Real Estate**: Provides steady appreciation and rental income but requires significant capital and maintenance.

- **Gold and Other Commodities**: Acts as a safe-haven investment, especially during economic uncertainty. However, price fluctuations can be unpredictable.

- **Art and Antiques**: Can deliver high returns, but their value depends on market trends and collector demand.

- **Vintage Cars**: Appreciates over time but requires care, maintenance, and knowledge of the industry.

2. Financial Assets

Financial assets represent ownership or a legal agreement that gives the holder the right to earn returns. These assets are generally more liquid than physical assets and can be easily converted into cash. Their value is based on market performance, company performance, or economic conditions.

Examples of Financial Assets:

- **Cash & Cash Equivalents**: Savings accounts, fixed deposits, and other equivalent investments provide security and liquidity but usually offer lower returns.

- **Stocks (Equities)**: Stocks represent ownership in a company. When you buy shares of a company, you become a shareholder and can benefit from price appreciation and dividends. The stock market is volatile, but over the long term, it has historically provided high returns.

- **Bonds**: Bonds are fixed-income instruments issued by governments or corporate entities. Investors earn interest on bonds, making them a stable investment with lower risk compared to stocks.

- **Mutual Funds/PMS/AIF/SIF**: It is a pool money from investors and invest in a diversified portfolio of stocks, bonds, or other assets. These investment vehicles are suitable for the investors who prefer professional management.

Performance of Financial Assets

- **Stocks/Private Equity**: High potential returns but come with market risk.

- **Bonds**: Lower risk, stable income, but limited growth potential.

- **Mutual Funds/PMS/AIF/SIF**: A balanced investment option, depending on the fund's composition.

- **Cash & Cash Equivalents**: Safe but provide low returns, often not keeping pace with inflation.

How to Choose the Right Asset Class for Investment?

Selecting the right asset class depends on various factors such as risk tolerance, investment goals, time horizon, and financial knowledge. Here are a few key considerations:

1. **Investment Objective:**

   - **Capital Appreciation:** If you aim to build long-term wealth, investing in stocks, real estate, or mutual funds is a better choice.

   - **Capital Preservation:** If preserving capital with minimal risk is the goal, bonds, fixed deposits and other such liquid assets are suitable options.

   - **Regular Income:** Rental properties, corporate fixed deposits, dividend-paying stocks, or bonds with regular interest can generate steady income.

2. Risk Appetite:

- **High Risk, High Return:** Stocks and commodities offer significant growth potential but come with market fluctuations.

- **Moderate Risk:** Mutual funds provide a balanced approach with diversified investments.

- **Low Risk, Low Return:** Bonds, bank deposits, and government securities are safer but yield lower returns.

3. Time Horizon:

- **Short-Term (0-3 years):** If you need liquidity in the short term, cash deposits and bonds are ideal.

- **Medium-Term (3-7 years):** Balanced mutual funds or a mix of bonds and stocks can offer stable growth.

- **Long-Term (7+ years):** Real estate, stocks, and equity-based mutual funds provide better returns over extended periods.

4. Market Conditions:

The economic environment plays a crucial role in asset performance. For example:

- During inflation, gold and real estate perform well.

- In a booming stock market, equities generate higher returns.

- When interest rates are high, fixed-income instruments like bonds become attractive.

5. Diversification Strategy:

It is always wise to diversify investments across multiple asset classes to spread risk. A balanced portfolio may include a mix of multiple or all of the above assets.

6. Ease of Acquisition & Liquidity:

Each asset class has unique characteristics that impact how easy it is to buy and sell, how much capital is required, and how quickly an investor can access their money. Each asset class differs based on seven key aspects: capital required as initial investment, ease of buying, time taken to buy, liquidity, time taken to sell, ease of selling, and diversification. This aspect has been explained in detail in chapter: 5 – Acquisition of an Asset & Liquidity.

Conclusion

Investment decisions should be based on careful evaluation of asset classes, performance trends, and personal financial goals. While physical assets like real estate and gold provide stability, financial assets such as stocks and bonds offer liquidity and growth potential. Diversification across different assets helps reduce risk and maximize returns. By understanding these asset classes and their characteristics, investors can make informed decisions that align with their financial aspirations and risk tolerance.

10-Point Summary: Where to Invest?

1. **Understanding Asset Classes** – Investments can be categorized into **physical assets** (real estate, commodities, collectibles) and **financial assets** (stocks, bonds, mutual funds, etc.), each with unique risks and benefits.

2. **Physical Assets** – Tangible assets like **real estate, gold, art, and vintage cars** offer stability, long-term appreciation, and inflation hedging but can be illiquid and require maintenance.

3. **Financial Assets** – Includes **stocks, bonds, mutual funds, and cash equivalents**, which provide liquidity and growth potential but are subject to market fluctuations.

4. **Performance of Physical Assets** – **Real estate and gold** are long-term wealth builders, **art and collectibles** depend on rarity and demand, and **vintage cars** appreciate with historical value.

5. **Performance of Financial Assets** – Stocks have high growth potential but are volatile, **bonds**

offer stable income with lower risk, and **mutual funds** provide diversification.

6. **Investment Objectives** – Choose assets based on goals:

   o **Capital Appreciation** – Stocks, real estate, and mutual funds.

   o **Capital Preservation** – Bonds and fixed deposits.

   o **Regular Income** – Rental properties, dividend stocks, and bonds.

7. **Risk Appetite** – Investments vary in risk:

   o **High Risk, High Return** – Stocks, commodities.

   o **Moderate Risk** – Mutual funds, mixed portfolios.

   o **Low Risk, Low Return** – Bonds, fixed deposits.

8. **Time Horizon** – Investment choices depend on duration:

   o **Short-term (0-3 years):** Cash, bonds.

   o **Medium-term (3-7 years):** Mutual funds, balanced portfolios.

   o **Long-term (7+ years):** Stocks, real estate, equity mutual funds.

9. **Market Conditions Impact** – Different assets perform better under various economic conditions:

   - **Inflation** – Gold, real estate.

   - **Stock Market Growth** – Equities.

   - **High-Interest Rates** – Bonds and fixed-income securities.

10. **Diversification Strategy** – Spreading investments across multiple asset classes reduces risk and enhances returns, ensuring a well-balanced portfolio aligned with financial goals.

Chapter: 3

Understanding Risk & It's Types: What Risk Factors to be Considered While Investment-decision Making?

Definition of Risk

Risk, in financial terms, represents the uncertainty of an investment's actual returns deviating from the expected outcome. It encompasses the potential loss of some or all of the initial investment. Every investor faces risk, making it a crucial factor in financial decision-making.

Largely, investment risk can be classified into two types:

1. **Absolute Risk**

2. **Relative Risk**

Both these risks influence investment decisions and portfolio management. Let's explore them in detail.

Absolute Risk

Absolute risk refers to the inherent potential for loss in an asset or portfolio, independent of market conditions or external influences. It focuses on the standalone performance of an investment, without any comparison to other assets or benchmarks. This type of risk is critical for investors who evaluate investments based on their individual performance metrics.

Examples of Absolute Risk

- **Volatility (Standard Deviation):** The price fluctuations of an asset over time indicate its volatility. A highly volatile investment has greater absolute risk.

- **Capital Loss Risk:** If the fundamental factors of an asset deteriorate, such as poor financial health of a company or declining market demand, the investor risks losing the principal investment.

Absolute risk is particularly relevant when investing in individual stocks, bonds, or alternative assets, where external factors do not influence the assessment of risk.

Relative Risk

Relative risk, on the other hand, considers how an investment's performance is influenced by external factors. This risk arises due to market conditions, economic trends, and industry-specific developments. Unlike absolute risk, relative risk is evaluated in comparison to a benchmark, such as an index or peer investments.

Examples of Relative Risk

- **Market Volatility:** The same standard deviation metric used in absolute risk can also be applied in relative terms when comparing an asset's volatility to the broader market or a sector index.

- **Sector-Specific Risks:** Investments in industries that are highly sensitive to external factors, such as oil prices for energy stocks or interest rate changes for financial stocks, carry relative risk. A decline in the industry can affect the value of related investments.

Investors managing diversified portfolios or index-based strategies pay close attention to relative risk, as it helps in understanding how an investment performs in comparison to others.

Managing Investment Risk

It is important to understand both absolute and relative risk as both are crucial in portfolio management. Investors often use strategies such as diversification, asset allocation, and risk assessment tools to mitigate risk and optimize returns.

- **Diversification:** Spreading investments across different asset classes reduces exposure to absolute and relative risks.

- **Risk-Adjusted Returns:** Metrics like the Sharpe Ratio and Beta help measure risk in relation to expected returns.

- **Hedging Strategies:** Using derivatives or alternative investments can help reduce risk exposure.

Conclusion

One should not avoid to understand the aspect of investment risk as it is a crucial part of financial decision-making. Absolute risk focuses on the inherent dangers of an individual asset, while relative risk considers the broader market impact. A well-balanced approach to risk assessment enables investors to make informed choices, safeguard their investments, and maximize potential returns.

10-Point Summary of Investment Risk Factors

1. **Definition of Risk** – Investment risk refers to the uncertainty of actual returns deviating from expected outcomes, potentially leading to partial or total loss of investment.

2. **Types of Risk** – Investment risk is broadly categorized into **absolute risk** (standalone asset

risk) and **relative risk** (risk in comparison to market conditions).

3. **Absolute Risk** – This refers to the inherent potential for loss in an asset, independent of external factors, focusing solely on its performance.

4. **Examples of Absolute Risk** – Includes **volatility** (price fluctuations over time) and **capital loss risk** (potential decline in an asset's fundamental value).

5. **Relative Risk** – This type of risk considers external influences such as market trends, economic conditions, and industry-specific factors.

6. **Examples of Relative Risk** – Includes **market volatility** (price movements in comparison to indices) and **sector-specific risks** (influences like oil prices on energy stocks).

7. **Risk Management Strategies** – Investors use **diversification** (spreading investments across asset classes) to mitigate absolute and relative risks.

8. **Risk-Adjusted Returns** – Metrics like the **Sharpe Ratio** (return per unit of risk) and **Beta** (volatility relative to the market) help assess investment risk.

9. **Hedging Strategies** – Techniques such as derivatives and alternative investments can be used to reduce exposure to market fluctuations.

10.**Balanced Risk Approach** – A comprehensive risk assessment helps investors make informed decisions, protect capital, and optimize returns.

Chapter: 4

Acquisition of Assets & Liquidity

To grow your wealth over time, investing is a great hack. However, not all investments are created equal. Each asset class has unique characteristics that impact how easy it is to buy and sell, how much capital is required, and how quickly an investor can access their money. In this chapter, we will compare different asset classes based on seven key aspects: capital required, ease of buying, time taken to buy, liquidity, time taken to sell, ease of selling, and diversification.

1. Capital Required to Buy an Asset

Different asset classes require different levels of initial investment. Let's take a look at some examples:

- **Stocks**: Investors can start with a small amount, even as little as Rs. 100. Many brokerages allow fractional share purchases, making it possible to invest in expensive stocks without needing a large sum of money.

- **Real Estate**: Buying property usually requires a substantial amount of capital. Even with mortgage financing, the down payment can be significant.

- **Bonds**: Government bonds can be purchased with relatively low capital, sometimes as little as Rs. 1000-Rs. 10,000. Corporate bonds may have higher minimum investment requirements.

- **Mutual Funds & ETFs**: These are great for investors, as many funds allow investments starting from as low as Rs. 500.

- **Gold & Precious Metals**: Physical gold can be expensive per unit, but gold ETFs allow investment with lower amounts.

- **Crypto currency**: Investors can start with very little money, often just a few dollars, making it one of the most accessible asset classes.

2. Ease of Buying

The ease of buying an asset depends on the process and availability.

- **Stocks, Mutual Funds, ETFs, and Crypto currencies**: These are among the easiest to buy, as they can be purchased through online brokerage accounts within minutes.

- **Bonds**: Buying government bonds is straightforward through banks or online platforms, but corporate bonds may require a broker.

- **Real Estate**: This is the most challenging asset to buy as it involves legal paperwork, financing, and sometimes lengthy negotiations.

- **Gold & Precious Metals**: Buying physical gold requires visiting a jeweller or bullion dealer, whereas gold ETFs can be purchased online.

3. **Time Taken to Buy**

- **Stocks, Mutual Funds, ETFs, and Crypto currencies**: Can be bought almost instantly through online platforms.

- **Bonds**: Government bonds can be bought quickly, but corporate bonds might take longer due to availability and approval processes.

- **Real Estate**: Can take weeks or even months due to inspections, loan approvals, and legal documentation.

- **Gold & Precious Metals**: Buying physical gold takes time for selection and verification, but gold ETFs are instant.

4. **Liquidity of the Asset**

When an asset can be easily converted into cash without significantly affecting its value is referred as liquidity.

- **Stocks & Crypto currencies**: Highly liquid assets that can be sold within seconds or minutes.

- **Mutual Funds & ETFs**: Fairly liquid as it takes 3 working days for the transaction to settle.

- **Bonds**: Some government bonds are liquid, but corporate bonds can take longer to sell.

- **Real Estate**: The most illiquid asset, as sale of property takes substantial time and effort.

- **Gold & Precious Metals**: Physical gold is somewhat liquid but requires a buyer and may involve price negotiations.

5. **Time Taken to Sell**

- **Stocks, Crypto currencies, Mutual Funds, and ETFs**: Can be sold almost instantly.

- **Bonds**: Government bonds can be sold quickly, while corporate bonds might take longer.

- **Real Estate**: Can take months due to listing, finding a buyer, and closing processes.

- **Gold & Precious Metals**: Can take a few hours or days, depending on where it is sold.

6. Ease of Selling

- **Stocks, Crypto currencies, Mutual Funds, and ETFs**: Easiest to sell through an online brokerage.

- **Bonds**: Easier to sell if government-issued but can be more challenging for corporate bonds.

- **Real Estate**: Selling property requires time, marketing, negotiations, and legal processes.

- **Gold & Precious Metals**: Selling to a jeweler or dealer is relatively simple but may involve price haggling.

7. Diversification Aspect

Diversification helps in risk management by spreading investments across different asset classes.

- **Stocks**: Investors can diversify by buying different companies, industries, and geographies.

- **Mutual Funds & ETFs**: Offer built-in diversification as they hold multiple assets.

- **Bonds**: Investing in bonds from different issuers (government, corporate) helps diversification.

- **Real Estate**: Harder to diversify as each property requires significant capital.

- **Gold & Precious Metals**: Generally not a diversified asset by itself, but it helps hedge against inflation.

- **Crypto currency**: Highly volatile but can be diversified by investing in different coins and tokens.

Conclusion

Each asset class has its unique characteristics. Equity shares, mutual funds, and Exchange traded funds offer high liquidity and ease of buying and selling. Real estate requires significant capital and time but can provide stability. Bonds offer safety, while gold act as hedging tool. A well-proportioned portfolio typically includes a mix of these asset classes to optimize returns while managing risks effectively. As an investor, understanding these aspects will help in making informed decisions and building a strong financial future.

Here's a 10-point summary of the content on *Acquisition of Assets & Liquidity:*

1. **Capital Requirements Vary across Assets**: Stocks, mutual funds, ETFs, and crypto require low capital to start, while real estate demands significant upfront investment.

2. **Ease of Buying Differs**: Stocks, ETFs, mutual funds, and crypto are easy to buy online; real estate

is the most complex due to paperwork and legal procedures.

3. **Buying Time Varies**: Digital assets like stocks and crypto can be bought instantly, whereas real estate transactions can take weeks or months.

4. **Liquidity Levels Are Unequal**: Stocks and crypto are highly liquid. Real estate and some corporate bonds are among the least liquid assets.

5. **Time to Sell Differs**: Stocks, mutual funds, and crypto can be sold quickly; real estate and certain bonds may take much longer to sell.

6. **Selling Ease is Asset Dependent**: Online platforms make selling stocks and ETFs simple, while selling property or corporate bonds involves more effort.

7. **Diversification Opportunities**: Mutual funds and ETFs offer built-in diversification. Real estate and gold offer limited diversification due to capital constraints or asset nature.

8. **Gold serves as a Hedge**: While not a diversified asset on its own, gold can hedge against inflation and add stability to a portfolio.

9. **Bonds Offer Safety with Limitations**: Government bonds are safer and relatively liquid; corporate bonds carry more risk and may be harder to trade.

10. **Balanced Portfolios Are Key**: A mix of asset classes helps balance risk and return. Understanding each asset's traits enables smarter investment decisions.

Chapter: 5

Our Behaviour Matters: Understanding the Edge in Investing

There was a time when information was scarce and hard to access. People had limited ways to gather and organize data, and very few possessed the resources to do so effectively. In those days, even basic corporate details like annual reports were shared only with shareholders, often in printed form. Some individuals took the initiative to collect such reports from multiple companies. They studied them carefully and used the insights gained to make smarter investment choices. These early investors had what we now refer to as an **Information Edge**—a unique advantage due to their access to information that wasn't readily available to everyone.

As technology progressed and awareness increased, information became more accessible. The once elusive edge of merely possessing data started to diminish. Now, more than just access to information, what set investors apart was their ability to interpret and analyze it. This marked the rise of the **Analytical Edge**. Those who could understand market trends, assess company performance, and derive meaning from raw data were able to generate higher returns than those who lacked analytical capabilities.

Fast forward to the present digital era. With the internet and advanced tools, data is available to virtually everyone at the click of a button. Be it financial reports, market analysis, or expert opinions—everything is within reach. In this landscape, both the information and analytical edge have become democratized. So, what gives an investor a real advantage today?

Behaviour

Yes, the differentiating factor now is how an investor behaves—particularly in response to market movements and emotional triggers like greed, fear, or impatience. This is what we call the **Behavioural Edge**.

Your success in investing depends not just on what you know or how well you analyze numbers, but significantly on **how you manage your emotions**, make decisions under pressure, and stick to your investment plan during turbulent times. In short, how you behave with your money matters more than ever.

The Three Sources of Alpha

In investment parlance, the term "Alpha" refers to the excess return that an investment generates over and above its expected performance. There are three broad sources of alpha:

1. **Information Alpha** – Gained by having superior access to valuable data.

2. **Analytical Alpha** – Earned through the ability to interpret that data better than others.

3. **Behavioural Alpha** – Derived from emotional discipline and sound financial behaviour.

In today's environment, behavioural alpha has emerged as the most critical of the three. Let's delve deeper into what shapes it.

The Role of Emotions: Greed and Fear

Two dominant emotions that shape financial decisions are **greed and fear**. Interestingly, these emotions often occur in cycles. After a market crash or a sharp decline, fear is high and people tend to withdraw or avoid investing. As the market recovers and begins to soar, greed kicks in, leading people to chase returns and pour money into already overvalued assets.

Recognizing this cycle presents an opportunity. When fear is peaking, it often signals a **buying opportunity**—a chance to invest at low valuations. When greed is dominant, it's a cue to be cautious, as the market might be approaching unsustainable highs.

Understanding and managing these emotional cycles can help you avoid impulsive decisions and instead follow a more calculated and disciplined investment strategy. This is the cornerstone of sound **investment behaviour**.

Behavioural Risk in Investing

When making an investment decision, people typically evaluate factors such as risk, potential returns, market trends, and volatility. While these are undoubtedly important, one key factor that is often overlooked is **the investor's own behaviour**.

We regularly tell clients: "Investments are subject to behavioural risk. Be mindful of your emotions before and during the investment process." Emotions influence decisions—whether it's overconfidence during a bull run or panic selling during a downturn.

By understanding our behavioural tendencies, we not only make more rational choices but also come to recognize the kind of investor we are. Based on practical experience and behavioural observation, investors can broadly be classified into five categories:

Investor Classifications: Who Are You?

Let's explore the five distinct investor types, along with relatable examples.

1. Passive Investor

This type sticks to a routine investment plan, such as regular monthly contributions through SIPs (Systematic Investment Plans), and avoids making any changes regardless of market conditions.

Example:

Mr. A invests ₹10,000 every month in mutual funds through SIPs for long-term wealth creation. Even when the market drops significantly, he continues his SIPs without attempting to invest more or withdraw funds.

2. Passive Investor with Active Interventions

These investors generally follow a passive approach but are willing to invest additional amounts when the market dips significantly to take advantage of lower valuations.

Example:

Mr. B also invests ₹10,000 monthly via SIPs. However, when markets correct by 20–30%, he invests an extra sum to average his cost and maximize long-term gains.

3. Strategic Investor

Strategic investors follow a predefined asset allocation plan tailored to their financial goals, time horizon, and risk tolerance. They periodically review and rebalance their portfolio based on their strategy.

Example:

Mr. C invests with a 25:75 debt-to-equity ratio. As he approaches retirement, he gradually shifts to a 75:25 debt-to-equity allocation to safeguard the corpus.

4. Tactical Investor

Tactical investors actively switch between asset classes based on market trends. Their approach is driven by short-term market dynamics and valuation-based decisions.

Example:

Mr. D invests entirely in equities when the market is undervalued. Once valuations rise significantly, he shifts his investments to debt. He constantly monitors market conditions to reallocate accordingly.

5. Vulnerable Investor

These investors tend to make emotional and convenience-based decisions. They often react impulsively to short-term performance and are more likely to chase trends or abandon investments prematurely.

Example:

Mr. E invests equally in five equity funds. When two of them underperform temporarily, he exits those funds out of fear and shifts to the three better-performing ones. Later, if another investment seems more promising, he again switches—chasing short-term performance.

Aligning Risk, Returns, and Goals

Identifying your investor type is crucial before choosing where to invest. For instance, while equity might help you achieve your goals faster with less capital, it may not be suitable if you lack the emotional resilience to withstand market volatility.

Often, people misclassify themselves—labelling themselves as aggressive investors based on hypothetical return comparisons across asset classes. But theoretical outcomes and actual behaviour during market turbulence are two very different things.

That's why **self-awareness** is key. Understanding your behavioural tendencies helps you build a portfolio aligned not just with your financial goals but also with your personality and risk appetite.

Even if you can't precisely identify your investor type at the beginning, it's important to develop this understanding early in your financial journey. Doing so helps you take thoughtful, measured steps instead of making emotionally driven decisions.

Final Thoughts: What Type of Investor Are You?

Now that you've explored these investor types and understood the concept of behavioural edge, take a moment to reflect. **Which category best describes you?** Are you a steady passive investor, a strategic planner, or do you find yourself reacting emotionally to every market swing?

Investing is more than just numbers and market trends—it's about managing your inner world. Your behaviour can either enhance or erode your returns. Cultivating discipline, patience, and self-awareness could very well be your most valuable investment.

So, ask yourself: *What kind of investor am I?* Your answer might just redefine your financial future.

Here's a 10-point summary of *"Our Behaviour Matters: Understanding the Edge in Investing"*:

1. **Evolution of Investment Edges**: Initially, investors gained an advantage through exclusive access to information (Information Edge). As access became widespread, the focus shifted to interpreting data (Analytical Edge). Today, the true differentiator is how investors behave—*the Behavioural Edge.*

2. **Information Is No Longer Exclusive**: With technological advancements and the internet, financial data and analysis are now accessible to all, eliminating the earlier advantage of information scarcity.

3. **Behavioural Edge Matters Most Today**: In the current era, emotional discipline and sound financial behaviour have become the primary sources of investment success, outweighing pure data access or analytical skills.

4. **Three Sources of Alpha**: Alpha, or excess returns, can come from:

   o   Information Alpha

   o   Analytical Alpha

   o   Behavioural Alpha (now the most critical one)

5. **Greed and Fear Drive Market Behaviour**: These two dominant emotions often cycle with the market. Recognizing these cycles can help investors act rationally—buying during fear and being cautious during greed.

6. **Behavioural Risk Is Real**: Emotional reactions like panic selling or overconfidence can lead to poor investment choices. Behavioural risk is often more impactful than market risk.

7. **Investor Types Identified**:

   o **Passive Investor**: Stays consistent regardless of market changes.

   o **Passive with Active Interventions**: Mostly passive but invests extra during market dips.

   o **Strategic Investor**: Follows and adjusts a long-term asset allocation strategy.

   o **Tactical Investor**: Actively shifts between assets based on market trends.

   o **Vulnerable Investor**: Reacts emotionally, often chasing returns or switching frequently.

8. **Know Your Investor Type**: Self-awareness helps you align your investments with your goals, risk tolerance, and emotional resilience, leading to better long-term outcomes.

9. **Behaviour Influences Portfolio Success**: Even the best strategies can fail if investors act impulsively. Consistent and disciplined behaviour is crucial to wealth creation.

10. **Reflection Is Key**: Understanding your behaviour and investor type is essential to becoming a better investor. The real edge lies not in beating the market—but in mastering yourself.

Chapter: 6

How Market and Economic Cycles Impact Investment Decision Making

The economy moves in cycles, much like the seasons. There are times of growth, times of decline, and everything in between. These cycles don't just affect businesses and governments—they shape human behaviour and influence investment decisions in powerful ways. Understanding these patterns can help investors make smarter choices and avoid common pitfalls.

The Four Phases of the Economic Cycle

The economic cycle consists of four main phases:

1. **Expansion** – The economy is growing, businesses are thriving, jobs are plentiful, and consumer confidence is high.

2. **Peak** – Growth reaches its highest point, but warning signs of overheating begin to appear.

3. **Recession** – Economic activity slows down, unemployment rises, and uncertainty spreads.

4. Trough – The economy hits the bottom, and a recovery process begins.

Each of these phases triggers different emotions and behaviours in people, affecting the way they invest.

How Economic Cycles Influence Human Behaviour

During Expansion: Optimism and Overconfidence

When the economy is booming, people feel good. They see rising stock markets, hear positive news, and feel secure about their jobs and finances. This optimism leads to increased spending and investment. Investors may become overconfident, believing that the market will continue to rise indefinitely.

Common Investor Mistakes:

- **Chasing high returns** – Buying assets at inflated prices, expecting them to keep going up.

- **Ignoring risks** – Underestimating potential downturns because everything looks positive.

- **Excessive borrowing** – Taking on debt to invest, assuming that prices will always rise.

At the Peak: Euphoria and Risk-Taking

At the peak of the economic cycle, excitement reaches its highest point. Many people enter the market, driven by the fear of missing out (FOMO). Speculation runs wild, and assets may be priced far beyond their actual value.

Common Investor Mistakes:

- **Herd mentality** – Following the crowd without conducting proper research.

- **Ignoring warning signs** – Dismissing economic indicators that suggest a slowdown is coming.

- **Overleveraging** – Taking excessive risks by investing borrowed money, which can lead to major losses when the market corrects.

During Recession: Fear and Panic

When the economy slows down, fear takes over. Stock prices fall, businesses struggle, and job losses rise. Investors who were once confident suddenly panic, selling their assets at low prices to cut their losses.

Common Investor Mistakes:

- **Selling in a panic** – Exiting the market at the worst possible time, locking in losses.

- **Short-term thinking** – Making decisions based on immediate fear rather than long-term goals.

- **Avoiding investment opportunities** – Staying out of the market even when prices become attractive.

At the Trough: Cautious Optimism and Missed Opportunities

As the economy begins to recover, some investors remain hesitant. They remember the pain of losses and fear another downturn. This cautious approach is natural but can also lead to missed opportunities.

Common Investor Mistakes:

- **Waiting too long** – Not investing early in the recovery phase, missing out on potential gains.

- **Distrust of markets** – Losing confidence in investments, leading to keeping money in low-return assets like cash.

- **Not rebalancing portfolios** – Failing to adjust investments according to new market conditions.

How to Make Smarter Investment Decisions

Understanding these cycles can help investors avoid emotional decision-making and focus on long-term success. Here are some key strategies:

1. **Stay Educated and Objective**

   Knowing that the market moves in cycles helps prevent emotional reactions. Instead of panicking during downturns or getting overexcited in booms, take a step back and assess the bigger picture.

2. Diversify Your Investments

A well-diversified portfolio can reduce risks during different economic phases. By spreading investments across different asset classes, sectors, and regions, you are less exposed to market volatility.

3. Stick to a Long-Term Plan

Short-term market movements can be unpredictable, but historical data shows that markets tend to rise over long periods. Staying committed to a well-thought-out investment strategy helps avoid costly mistakes.

4. Avoid Emotional Decision-Making

Making investment decisions based on fear or greed often leads to poor outcomes. Using logic, research, and professional advice can help maintain a rational approach.

5. Take Advantage of Market Downturns

Recessions and bear markets can be excellent opportunities to buy high-quality assets at discounted prices. Instead of selling in fear, smart investors look for bargains.

6. Regularly Rebalance Your Portfolio

Market conditions change, and so should your investments. Rebalancing ensures that your portfolio stays aligned with your goals and risk tolerance.

Conclusion

Market and economic cycles are natural, and they play a significant role in shaping human behaviour and investment decisions. By recognizing how emotions influence decision-making, investors can avoid common pitfalls and make better choices. Staying informed, maintaining a long-term perspective, and practicing disciplined investing can help navigate these cycles successfully, leading to financial growth and stability.

10-Point Summary: How Market and Economic Cycles Impact Investment Decision-Making

1. **Economic Cycles Influence Investments** – The economy moves in cycles (Expansion, Peak, Recession, and Trough), affecting investor behavior and decision-making.

2. **Expansion Phase** – During economic growth, optimism prevails, leading to increased investment and spending. Investors may chase high returns, underestimate risks, and take on excessive debt.

3. **Peak Phase** – Excitement and speculation dominate, causing overvaluation of assets. Common mistakes include herd mentality, ignoring warning signs, and excessive risk-taking with borrowed money.

4. **Recession Phase** – Fear and panic lead to declining stock prices and economic uncertainty. Investors may sell in panic, focus on short-term losses, and avoid investment opportunities.

5. **Trough Phase** – As recovery begins, investors remain cautious, potentially missing opportunities. Common errors include waiting too long to reinvest, distrusting markets, and failing to adjust portfolios.

6. **Emotions Drive Investment Mistakes** – Psychological factors like fear, greed, and overconfidence influence decisions, often leading to poor investment choices.

7. **Importance of Diversification** – A well-balanced portfolio across asset classes, sectors, and regions helps mitigate risks in different economic phases.

8. **Long-Term Strategy is Key** – Staying committed to a long-term investment plan helps navigate short-term market volatility and avoid reactionary decisions.

9. **Taking Advantage of Downturns** – Economic downturns present opportunities to buy undervalued assets, allowing investors to benefit from eventual recoveries.

10. **Regular Portfolio Rebalancing** – Adjusting investments periodically ensures alignment with financial goals and changing market conditions, improving long-term success.

Chapter: 7

Alignment of Goals:
The Financial Life Cycle

Introduction

Every individual, family, or business entity embarks on a financial journey that follows a structured life cycle. Understanding this cycle can help in making informed financial decisions and achieving long-term financial security by aligning financial goals effectively. The financial life cycle consists of five key stages:

1. **Earning**

2. **Protection**

3. **Goal Planning**

4. **Wealth Creation**

5. **Legacy Planning**

Each stage plays a crucial role in building financial stability and securing the future. Let's explore these stages in detail.

Stage 1: Start Earning

The foundation of financial planning begins with earning. Whether you are an individual, a family, or a business, generating income is the first step. The focus should then shift towards increasing net earnings, which can be defined as:

Net Earnings = Income - Expenses - Taxes

As income grows, financial aspirations naturally emerge. These may include buying a dream home, owning a luxury car, starting a business, funding a child's education abroad, or traveling the world. However, before pursuing these aspirations, it is vital to safeguard financial well-being.

Stage 2: Protection - Securing Your Finances

Financial protection is the first step in responsible financial planning. It ensures that unforeseen events do not cause financial distress to you, your family, or your business. The key question to ask is: **"Am I adequately protected?"**

Protection in financial terms means **insurance**. Adequate insurance coverage is essential and should be prioritized as follows:

1. **Personal Accident & Loss of Income Cover** – To secure income in case of disability or accidents.

2. **Life Insurance** – To ensure financial security for dependents.

3. **Health Insurance** – To cover medical emergencies and expenses.

4. **Asset Insurance** – To protect valuable assets such as homes, vehicles, and business properties.

5. **Liability Insurance** – To safeguard against legal and public liabilities.

By setting these priorities, one can design an annual insurance plan and allocate a budget accordingly. Once adequate protection is in place, the next step is to assess financial surplus and channel it towards goal planning.

Stage 3: Goal Planning - Turning Dreams into Reality

Once protection is ensured, the focus shifts to setting and achieving financial goals. Goals can vary based on personal or business aspirations:

For Individuals & Families:

- Purchasing a dream home

- Buying a luxury car

- Saving for a child's higher education

- Funding a child's wedding

- Traveling abroad or going on a world tour

- Creating a contingency fund

- Building a retirement corpus

For Businesses & Companies:

- Accumulating funds for future asset purchases

- Investing in research and development

- Managing short-term liabilities

- Preserving funds from advances

- Expanding operations

- Covering contingent liabilities

Setting a Timeline for Goals

Every financial goal should have a timeline:

- **Short-term goals** (up to 3 years)

- **Medium-term goals** (3 to 7 years)

- **Long-term goals** (beyond 7 years)

Goal planning involves identifying what you want to achieve and mapping out a structured plan with **SMART objectives** (Specific, Measurable, Achievable, Relevant, and Time-bound).

Stage 4: Wealth Creation - Growing Your Financial Future

After securing insurance and setting goals, any remaining surplus can be directed towards **wealth**

creation. Wealth creation is about making strategic investments to generate long-term financial growth.

Example Calculation:

- **Net Earnings:** ₹100

- **Annual Insurance Expenses:** ₹30

- **Goal Planning Allocation:** ₹40

- **Final Surplus:** ₹30

This remaining surplus is what we call **Risk Capital**, which can be invested in high-risk, high-return assets such as:

- Equity markets

- Mutual funds

- Startups and business ventures

- Real estate investments

However, wealth creation should not be confused with gambling. Thoughtful planning and calculated risk-taking can accelerate financial freedom and even lead to **FIRE (Financial Independence, Retire Early).**

Stage 5: Legacy Planning - Ensuring Continuity

At a certain stage in life, it becomes important to plan for the transfer of wealth to the next generation. Legacy planning ensures that assets are distributed as per your wishes and business continuity is secured.

Key elements of legacy planning include:

1. **Preparing a will or estate plan**

2. **Structuring asset transfers to legal heirs**

3. **Planning business succession**

By having a well-defined legacy plan, one can ensure a smooth transition of wealth and prevent future legal complications.

Conclusion

Financial planning is a structured journey that begins with earning, securing, and planning, followed by wealth creation and legacy planning. By following this systematic approach, individuals and businesses can achieve financial stability, independence, and long-term prosperity.

Here's a 10-point summary of the financial life cycle chapter:

1. **Financial Life Cycle Stages** – The journey includes five key stages: Earning, Protection, Goal Planning, Wealth Creation, and Legacy Planning.

2. **Earning Stage** – The foundation of financial planning starts with generating income and

managing net earnings (Income – Expenses – Taxes).

3. **Protection Stage** – Securing finances through various insurances (life, health, accident, asset, and liability) to mitigate financial risks.

4. **Goal Planning** – Setting financial goals based on personal and business aspirations, categorized into short-term (up to 3 years), medium-term (3-7 years), and long-term (beyond 7 years).

5. **SMART Goal Setting** – Goals should be Specific, Measurable, Achievable, Relevant, and Time-bound to ensure financial success.

6. **Wealth Creation** – Investing surplus funds in high-return opportunities such as equity, mutual funds, start-ups, and real estate for long-term financial growth.

7. **Risk Capital** – The remaining surplus after expenses, insurance, and goal planning should be strategically invested rather than gambled.

8. **FIRE Concept** – Financial Independence, Retire Early (FIRE) can be achieved through careful financial planning and disciplined wealth creation.

9. **Legacy Planning** – Ensuring smooth wealth transfer through wills, asset structuring, and business succession planning.

10.**Financial Stability & Prosperity** – Following this structured financial life cycle enables individuals and businesses to achieve financial security, independence, and long-term wealth.

Chapter: 8

The 9 Factor Model Summary

After a thorough understanding of different aspects of investing, you have a detailed answer for each of the following questions:

1. Where should we invest?

2. What return can we expect?

3. What is the cost of investment?

4. What risks are involved?

5. How easily can we acquire the investment?

6. How easy is it to exit from the investment?

7. How should we behave with our investments?

8. Why are we investing in the first place?

9. How do the market and economy affect our investment?

This helps you to eliminate any ambiguity before & during your investment journey, enables you to make decisions with clarity and helps in making your money work for you. This chapter summarizes all the earlier chapters and thereby devises a go-to model for your operational ease.

Here's a ready reckoner of all the factors:

1. Asset

- Equity, Debt, Real Estate, Art Works, Gold or other commodities etc. - Each asset yields different return on investment.

- Mutual Funds, PMS, AIFs, Direct Equity etc - Each investment vehicle has different style & mode of investing.

- Picking up a right asset class & investment vehicle is important

2. Return on Investment (ROI)

- An asset can generate regular income or capital appreciation or both.

- What return can be expected depends on what asset class/investment vehicle you choose.

3. Cost of Investment

- Cost of Acquiring + Cost of Holding + Cost of Sale/Transfer = Total Cost of Investment

- Real ROI = Return on Investment - Cost of Investment

4. Risk Involved

- Two types of risk are involved: Absolute Risk & Relative Risk

- "Absolute risk" refers to the inherent risk of a specific investment or portfolio, measured independently without comparison to a benchmark.

- "Relative risk" compares the risk of an investment to a reference point like a market index

5. Capital Requirement

- This refers to ease of buying an asset or ease of investing.

- Eg.: Suppose Rs. 50 Lakhs is required to buy one house property while with the same amount you can build a diversified equity portfolio or buy a PMS/Mutual Funds.

6. Liquidity

- This refers to ease of selling an asset or ease of exit from investment.

- Suppose your total investment is Rs. 50 Lakhs. Now imagine if there is a contingency situation and you need Rs. 10 Lakhs. Understand, which asset class offers you the ease of exit & in what time!

7. Market & Economic Cycle

- Each asset class has a periodic pattern of growth & decline due to multiple factors.

- Understanding this cyclicality, helps in finding buying opportunity, accumulation and diversification of investment.

8. Alignment with Goals

- At the time of investing, it is great to have a clarity of when will you require the money back and for what purpose.

- Simply, this helps you have a good sleep as compared to keeping your investment ambiguous.

9. Behaviour

- After understanding all the above technicalities, you may not be able to generate expected returns IF you do not behave wisely with your money.

- Do not let your emotions drive your investments. Mind you, this majorly contributes in your wealth creation. IT IS CALLED BEHAVIOURAL ALPHA.

By using these factors, you are equipped with a model for making your investment decisions and thus this is known as **9 Factor Model** for making investment decision. This will ensure you behave rationally while investing and enables you to make informed decision.

Chapter: 9

The Art of Asset Allocation

While building a sound investment portfolio, asset allocation is a foundational element. It provides a framework for balancing risk and return, aligning strategies to individual or institutional goals and adapting to dynamic market conditions. This chapter explains the principles and considerations involved in designing effective investment portfolio.

What is Asset Allocation?

Asset allocations refers to distribution of investment across different asset classes to optimize returns while managing risk. The primary goal is to balance risk and reward based on an individual's financial goals, risk tolerance, and investment horizon. Think of asset allocation as the blueprint of your portfolio.

The Importance of Asset Allocation

Each asset class has different characteristics. Each of them has unique risk and return profile as we have already understood. Thus, having an absolute exposure or majority exposure to a single asset class can put your money to risk. In the world of investing, it is not only important to ensure that your portfolio is well positioned for growth but also protected from undue risk.

The rationale behind asset allocation lies in diversification. By spreading investment across assets that respond differently to economic factors, investor can mitigate volatility and improve risk return trade-off. For instance, during period of stock market turbulence, bonds might provide stability, while alternative assets like commodities can hedge against inflation.

The Role of Risk Tolerance & Time Horizon

Your asset allocation should reflect your **risk tolerance** (how much volatility you can handle emotionally and financially) and **time horizon** (how long until you need the money).

- A young investor saving for retirement 30 years away can afford a more aggressive allocation tilted toward equities.

- A retiree relying on their portfolio for income may prefer a conservative allocation with more bonds and cash.

It's not about avoiding risk but aligning risk with your goals.

Strategic vs. Tactical Asset Allocation

Two ways to approach asset allocation:

- **Strategic Asset Allocation:** It is a long term approach. You can set a target allocation (Example: 70% Equity, 20% Bonds, 10% Gold) and rebalance it periodically to maintain that proportion, irrespective of market fluctuations. Another idea is to align your investments with time horizon (Example: Short term investments are parked in low duration bonds, long term investments are allocated to equity).

- **Tactical Asset Allocation:** This is an active approach based on market conditions. For instance, if stocks seem overvalued, you might temporarily shift more to cash or bonds. Once market valuations get cheaper, you shift from bonds or cash to equity. This can also be termed as dynamic asset allocation approach.

Strategic asset allocation tends to outperform in the long run due to its discipline and lower costs. Tactical allocation is used to seize short term opportunities and continuous application of the same tends to have higher cost which would hamper the effective rate of return on investment.

What is Diversification?

It is a practice of spreading your money within and across different asset classes. The logic is simple: don't put all your eggs in one basket.

Within each asset class, you can diversify further:

- **Equities:** Invest in different sectors (technology, healthcare, consumer goods), regions (U.S., Europe, emerging markets), and market capitalizations (large-cap, mid-cap, small-cap).

- **Bonds:** Spread across corporate, municipal, government, and international bonds, with varying durations and credit qualities.

- **Real Estate:** Own properties in different geographic locations and different types (residential, commercial, and industrial).

Diversification is not just limited to asset class. You can diversify your investment portfolio with exposure to different geographies as well as different currencies.

The aim is to build a portfolio where the performance of one investment doesn't overly influence the total outcome. When one asset zigs, another might zag, helping to smooth returns.

The Power of Low Correlation

At the heart of diversification is the concept of **correlation**—how assets move in relation to each other. A correlation of +1 means assets move in lockstep, while -1 means they move in opposite directions.

For diversification to be effective, you want assets with **low or negative correlations**. This is why pairing stocks with bonds works well: when markets fall, bonds often hold steady or rise, cushioning the blow.

During times of crisis, correlations can increase temporarily—many assets fall together—but a diversified portfolio still performs better than a concentrated one over time.

The Myth of Over Diversification

There is such a thing as too much diversification—commonly known as **diversification**. Spreading investments across too many assets can dilute potential returns without providing much additional risk reduction.

For example, owning 100 different stocks doesn't significantly reduce your risk compared to owning 20 carefully chosen ones across sectors and geographies. At some point, adding more assets increases complexity without proportionate benefit.

The key is **thoughtful diversification**—choosing assets that play distinct roles and complement each other within the portfolio.

Rebalancing: Staying on Track

Over time, market movements will alter your original asset allocation. For instance, if stocks perform well, they might grow from 60% to 70% of your portfolio, increasing your overall risk exposure.

Rebalancing is the process of realigning your portfolio to its target allocation. This can be done:

- **Periodically** (e.g., once a year)
- **Threshold-based** (e.g., when an asset deviates by more than 5%)

Rebalancing forces you to sell high and buy low—a discipline that can enhance long-term performance and maintain your risk profile.

Asset Allocation across Life Stages

Your ideal allocation changes over your lifetime. Here's a general framework:

1. **Early Career (20s-30s):** Focus on growth. High equity exposure (80–90%) makes sense due to a long time horizon and ability to recover from volatility.

2. **Mid-Career (40s-50s):** Start dialling back risk. A mix of 60–70% equities with some bonds and alternatives for stability is common.

3. **Pre-Retirement (50s-60s):** Prioritize preservation. Reduce equity exposure to 50–60% and increase bonds and cash to buffer against market downturns.

4. **Retirement (60s+):** Focus on income and capital preservation. A balanced mix of income-generating assets, including bonds, dividend-paying stocks, and possibly annuities, is appropriate.

Asset Allocation in Practice: Model Portfolios

Here are a few simplified model allocations:

Aggressive Portfolio (Growth Focus):

- 80% Equities (including international and small caps)

- 10% Bonds

- 10% Alternatives or Cash

Moderate Portfolio (Balanced):

- 60% Equities

- 30% Bonds

- 10% Cash/Alternatives

Conservative Portfolio (Capital Preservation):

- 30% Equities

- 50% Bonds

- 20% Cash/Stable Value Assets

These are starting points—customization is key based on your unique needs.

Diversification in a Global World

Investors today are not limited to domestic markets. **Global diversification** has become a key strategy. Different regions and countries have distinct economic cycles, currencies, and growth prospects.

Investing in international assets—be it emerging markets or developed economies—adds another layer of protection and opportunity. However, it also introduces foreign exchange risk and geopolitical considerations, which should be managed carefully.

The Behavioural Benefits of Diversification

Diversification isn't just about reducing risk—it also helps **manage emotions**. Market volatility can provoke fear and panic-selling. A diversified portfolio acts as a stabilizer, helping investors stay the course and avoid destructive decisions.

Knowing that some parts of your portfolio are designed to withstand downturns can provide the psychological comfort needed to maintain discipline during turbulent times.

Conclusion: Building a Portfolio for the Long Haul

Asset allocation and diversification are not flashy concepts, but they are powerful. They don't promise instant riches or market-beating returns. Instead, they offer something far more valuable: **resilience**.

By thoughtfully spreading your investments across asset classes and rebalancing over time, you position yourself to weather storms and capture opportunities. This approach won't always outperform in the short term, but it is your best ally in the pursuit of sustainable, long-term wealth.

Here's a 10-point summary of *The Art of Asset Allocation:*

Foundation of Portfolio Building: Asset allocation is a critical strategy for balancing risk and return while aligning investments with financial goals and adapting to market conditions.

1. **Definition & Purpose**: It involves distributing investments across various asset classes (like equities, bonds, real estate, etc.) to optimize returns and manage risk based on risk tolerance, goals, and time horizon.

2. **Importance of Diversification**: Diversifying across and within asset classes helps reduce portfolio volatility and enhances the risk-return profile by ensuring that poor performance in one area can be offset by others.

3. **Role of Risk Tolerance & Time Horizon**: Your ideal allocation depends on how much risk you can emotionally and financially handle and how long you can stay invested—longer horizons often allow for higher equity exposure.

4. **Strategic vs. Tactical Approaches**:

   ○ *Strategic Asset Allocation* is a long-term, disciplined approach based on maintaining fixed proportions.

   ○ *Tactical Asset Allocation* is more dynamic and responsive to market conditions, but it often involves higher costs and complexity.

5. **Low Correlation is Key**: Effective diversification requires low or negative correlation between asset classes so they don't all move in the same direction during market events.

6. **Beware of Over-Diversification**: Spreading too thin across many assets can reduce potential gains and complicate management without adding significant risk reduction.

7. **Rebalancing for Discipline**: Periodic rebalancing keeps your portfolio aligned with your original allocation and helps manage risk by encouraging buy-low, sell-high behavior.

8. **Lifecycle-Based Allocation**: Asset allocation should evolve with age—from growth-focused in early career to income-focused and risk-averse in retirement.

9. **Global & Behavioral Edge**: Incorporating global assets increases diversification benefits but comes with currency and geopolitical risks. Diversification also provides psychological comfort during market downturns, helping investors avoid panic-driven decisions.

Chapter: 10

The Magic of Compounding: How Time Turns Small Steps Into Big Rewards

Imagine a tiny snowball rolling down a hill. At first, it's just a handful of snow. But as it rolls, it gathers more snow. With every turn, it grows — slowly at first, then rapidly. By the time it reaches the bottom of the hill, it's a giant ball of snow, all from that small start.

That, in essence, is compounding.

Compounding is one of the most powerful forces in the financial world. It's simple, almost boring at first glance — but once you truly understand how it works, you'll see why Albert Einstein reportedly called it the "eighth wonder of the world."

In this chapter, we'll break down the concept of compounding, explore how it works, and show you why starting early (even with small amounts) can make a huge difference. By the end, you'll have a new appreciation for time and patience when it comes to money.

What Is Compounding?

Let's start with the basics. Compounding is the process where the earnings on your money begin to earn their own earnings.

Put another way: you earn interest not just on your original amount, but also on the interest that you've already earned.

Here's a quick example:

Suppose you invest ₹1,000 at a 10% annual interest rate.

- **After 1 year:** You'll have ₹1,100 (your original ₹1,000 plus ₹100 interest).

- **After 2 years:** You'll earn 10% on ₹1,100 — giving you ₹1,210.

- **After 3 years:** Your money becomes ₹1,331 — because now you're earning interest on ₹1,210, not just your original ₹1,000.

The extra money you earn from interest earning more interest — *that's* the magic of compounding.

The Two Ingredients of Compounding: Time and Rate

Compounding works best with two main ingredients:

1. **Time**

2. **Rate of return**

Let's unpack each.

1. Time

Time is the most powerful ally of compounding. The longer your money stays invested, the more compounding can work its magic. Even if the returns aren't huge every year, over time they snowball into something significant.

Consider this:

- ₹1,000 is invested at 10% annual interest, in **10 years** it becomes ₹2,593.

- In **20 years**, it grows to ₹6,727.

- In **30 years**, it becomes ₹17,449.

- In **50 years**, it's a massive ₹117,390.

The same ₹1,000, just left to grow — no extra contributions needed.

The big jump in later years shows the real power of compounding. It starts slowly, then picks up momentum. That's why **starting early** is the key to building wealth.

2. Rate of Return

The rate of return also matters. Even small increases in returns can make a big difference over long periods.

Let's say two people invest ₹10,000 for 30 years:

- One earns **6% annual return**: they end up with ₹57,435.

- Another earns **8% return**: they get ₹1,00,627.

- At **10% return**, it becomes ₹1,74,494.

That's a difference of nearly ₹1.2 lakh between 6% and 10%, all because of compounding working harder at a higher rate.

Of course, higher returns often come with more risk — but this shows why choosing the right investments is important.

The Power of Starting Early

Here's a story of two sisters: Riya and Richa.

- **Richa** starts investing ₹5,000 a month at age 25 and stops after 10 years (so she invests ₹6,00,000 total).

- **Riya** starts at 35 and invests ₹5,000 a month until she's 60 (₹15,00,000 total).

Assuming a 10% return:

- At age 60, **Richa** has ₹95 lakhs.

- **Riya**, despite investing 2.5 times more, ends up with only ₹95 lakhs as well.

Richa's early start gave her compounding power. She stopped investing after 10 years, but her money kept growing. Time was her biggest asset.

Moral? **Start as early as you can.**

Compound Interest vs. Simple Interest

Let's quickly look at the difference.

- **Simple interest**: You earn interest only on the original principal.

- **Compound interest**: You earn interest on the principal *and* the interest earned.

Example: ₹1,000 at 10% interest for 3 years.

- **Simple interest**: You get ₹100 each year → Total = ₹1,300.

- **Compound interest**: You get ₹100 in year 1, ₹110 in year 2, ₹121 in year 3 → Total = ₹1,331.

Not a huge difference in 3 years. But stretch that over 20–30 years, and compound interest leaves simple interest in the dust.

The Rule of 72

Want to know how long it'll take your money to double? Use the **Rule of 72**.

Just divide 72 by your interest rate.

- At 6% return → $72 \div 6 = 12$ years to double.

- At 9% return → $72 \div 9 = 8$ years to double.

- At 12% return → $72 \div 12 = 6$ years to double.

It's a quick and handy way to understand how compounding works at different rates.

Common Places Where Compounding Works

Compounding isn't just for savings accounts. You'll find it working in many areas:

1. **Stock Market**

   Investing in good companies and holding for the long term lets compounding play out. The stock market can be volatile in the short term, but over decades, it has created huge wealth.

2. **Mutual Funds**

   SIP (Systematic Investment Plan) in mutual funds is a great way to take advantage of compounding. Regular monthly investments, combined with the power of time, work wonders.

3. **Retirement Accounts**

   EPF, NPS, PPF — all of these use compounding. Leaving your retirement money untouched for years helps it grow substantially.

4. **Fixed Deposits and Bonds**

   Even in safer instruments like FDs and bonds, reinvesting the interest can create compounding effects.

Why People Miss Out on Compounding

If compounding is so amazing, why don't more people benefit from it?

Here are a few reasons:

1. Starting Late

Many people wait until their 30s or 40s to start saving. By then, they've lost years where compounding could've worked for them.

2. Interruptions

Frequent withdrawals break the compounding cycle. If you keep dipping into your savings, your future growth suffers.

3. Lack of Patience

Compounding needs time. People want quick results, and when they don't see big gains in the first few years, they give up.

4. Low Returns

Keeping money in low-interest accounts like a regular savings account limits the power of compounding.

Tips to Make Compounding Work for You

1. **Start Now**: There is no perfect time. Start with whatever you can, even if it's just ₹500 per month.

2. **Be Consistent**: Regular investing beats occasional big investments.

3. **Reinvest Your Earnings**: Let your interest/ dividends stay invested.

4. **Stay Invested for the Long Term**: Time is your best friend.

5. **Avoid Withdrawals**: Let the money grow uninterrupted.

6. **Increase Contributions Over Time**: As your income grows, increase your investment amount.

Compounding Beyond Money

Compounding isn't just about money. It works in other areas of life too.

1. **Learning**

    Reading a few pages daily compounds your knowledge over time. A small habit, consistently followed, makes you smarter.

2. **Health**

    Exercising 20 minutes a day might not seem like much — but over months and years, it leads to huge fitness gains.

3. Relationships

Spending quality time with loved ones, consistently, deepens bonds over time. It's a form of emotional compounding.

The idea is simple: **Small things, done regularly, produce big results over time.**

Conclusion: Trust the Process

Compounding is slow magic. In the beginning, it might seem like nothing's happening. But give it time, and it can turn modest efforts into extraordinary outcomes.

You don't need a big salary or fancy degrees to benefit from compounding. What you need is:

- A willingness to start early
- The patience to stay the course
- The discipline to be consistent

Whether it's ₹100 or ₹10,000 a month — just begin. Let compounding do its work. One day, you'll look back and be amazed at how far your money (and your efforts) have come.

Remember the snowball? Start rolling yours today.

Here's a 10-point summary of *The Magic of Compounding: How Time Turns Small Steps into Big Rewards:*

What is Compounding?

Compounding is when your investments earn returns, and those returns begin to earn returns themselves — like a snowball gathering more snow as it rolls.

2. Power Ingredients: Time & Rate of Return

The two key factors that make compounding work are **time** (the longer your money stays invested, the better) and **rate of return** (even small increases can lead to big differences over time).

3. Start Early, Reap More

Starting early — even with smaller amounts — gives compounding more time to work. A few early years can outweigh larger investments made later.

4. Real-Life Example: Richa vs. Riya

Richa invested for 10 years starting at 25, while Riya invested for 25 years starting at 35. Despite investing less money, Richa ended up with the same amount — thanks to time and compounding.

5. Compound vs. Simple Interest

Simple interest earns only on the original amount. Compound interest earns on both the principal and the accumulated interest — creating a much larger impact over time.

6. Rule of 72

A quick trick to estimate how long it takes for your money to double: divide 72 by the interest rate. For example, at 6% return, money doubles in 12 years.

7. Where Compounding Works

Compounding can be harnessed through investments like stocks, mutual funds (SIPs), retirement accounts (PPF, EPF, NPS), and reinvested fixed deposits.

8. Why People Miss Out

Common mistakes include starting late, withdrawing funds early, being impatient, and settling for low-return instruments that limit compounding power.

9. Tips to Maximize Compounding

Start now, invest consistently, reinvest your earnings, stay invested long-term, avoid early withdrawals, and increase contributions as your income grows.

10. Beyond Finance: Life Compounds Too

Compounding applies to learning, health, and relationships. Small, consistent actions — like daily reading or exercise — produce exponential benefits over time.

Chapter: 11

Rupee Cost Averaging

As we have understood, markets are cyclical in nature both; in short term as well as long term. In addition to this, assets are also affected by inherent and external market factors. This causes price fluctuations which results in volatility. As a lay investor, volatility may concern you. However, volatility is a boon to an investor.

Let us take an example:

Suppose you have an ice-cream shop and you need mangoes to make mango flavoured ice-cream. You buy mangoes on weekly basis.

Week 1 – Price: Rs. 100 per Kg

Week 2 – Price: Rs. 115 per Kg

Week 3 – Price: Rs. 95 per Kg

To save on cost, it is quite obvious that you would like to buy and store mangoes at a cheaper rate. Hence, you would buy more mangoes in week 3 and store the same for future use. Buying more at cheaper rate averages out your total cost and assuming that your selling price remains unchanged, you will have better profitability on sale of mango ice-cream.

The same logic applies to investing as well.

There are several investment instruments such as mutual funds, exchange traded funds, stocks where a facility of systematic investment plan (SIP) is available. SIP helps you capitalize on rupee cost averaging.

Following example will explain the concept clearly:

Richa invests a fixed amount of Rs. 10000 every month with an SIP in a mutual fund scheme. Let's look at two scenarios – When market goes higher & when market falls. Assuming that she started investing and market went up for 8 months.

Month	Amount Invested each month	Price per unit	No. of Units Accumulated
1	1000	15	66.66
2	1000	16.5	60.60
3	1000	18.3	54.64
4	1000	22	45.45
5	1000	24.6	40.65
6	1000	25	40
7	1000	28.1	35.59
8	1000	29	34.48
Total	**8000**		**378.07**

The average cost of buying each unit in this case comes at a much lower Rs 21.16 (total amount invested/

total units accumulated). Similarly, if we assume that the markets fall during the 8 months, the average cost of each unit would come to Rs 20.05.

Month	Amount Invested each month	Price per unit	No. of Units Accumulated
1	1000	27	37.03
2	1000	25.5	39.21
3	1000	23	43.48
4	1000	21.6	46.29
5	1000	20.1	49.75
6	1000	18.5	54.05
7	1000	16	62.5
8	1000	15	66.67
Total	8000		398.98

In the second (market falling) scenario, if Richa would have invested Rs 8,000 as lump sum in April itself at a NAV of Rs 27, then she would have got 296.29 units. These units by the end of 7 months would have brought down Richa's investment value to just Rs 4,444.35 (296.29 units multiplied by price of each unit in November, i.e. Rs 15).

Comparing this to 398.98 units accumulated using the rupee cost averaging approach, her investment value in this case would be Rs 5,984.7. One can clearly see the difference rupee cost averaging has made in cutting losses in Richa's investment.

Importance of Rupee Cost Averaging:

1. Mitigating Volatility Risk

    The primary benefit is the ability to mitigate the impact of price volatility. If you invest a fixed amount at regular intervals, you can get more units when the prices are lower and fewer units when prices are high. This reduces the risk of making significant investment at wrong time.

2. Disciplined Investing

    Systematic investing makes your capital deployment automatic. This indirectly inculcates a discipline of regular investing. Discipline and consistency are the key factors for long term wealth creation.

3. Emotional Control

    Fall in market can make you hesitant in investing money during that phase. It is quite natural to have a fear while investing in falling market. However price fall brings in opportunity to buy more. Rupee cost averaging removes the need for emotional decision making. Irrespective of market condition, you keep investing systematically, which helps you in avoiding impulsive decision making. Your decision are not driven by greed or fear. More importantly, this approach brings automation in investing.

4. Power of Compounding

When the aim is to accumulate wealth and long term wealth creation, rupee cost averaging is considered ideal. Over a longer time horizon, the power of compounding along with discipline, has a potential to grow your investments multifold.

Conclusion:

Rupee Cost Averaging (RCA) is a powerful and practical investment strategy, especially for individuals navigating the uncertainties of the market. As we've seen, markets fluctuate due to various factors, but instead of fearing volatility, investors can harness it to their advantage. By investing a fixed amount regularly, regardless of market conditions, you not only average out your purchase cost but also develop financial discipline, avoid emotional decision-making, and benefit from the long-term power of compounding.

Whether markets are rising or falling, RCA ensures that your investment journey remains steady and consistent. It is not about timing the market, but rather about spending time in the market — systematically and patiently. For anyone aiming to build long-term wealth while minimizing the impact of volatility, rupee cost averaging offers a simple yet effective path forward.

Here's a 10-point summary of the concept of Rupee Cost Averaging (RCA):

1. **Markets Are Volatile**: Financial markets fluctuate due to cyclical trends and external factors, leading to price volatility.

2. **Volatility as an Opportunity**: Rather than fearing volatility, investors can use it to their advantage by buying more when prices are low and less when prices are high.

3. **Analogy with Mango Prices**: Just as one would buy more mangoes when they're cheaper to average out costs and increase profits, the same principle applies to investing.

4. **Systematic Investment Plan (SIP)**: SIPs in mutual funds and similar instruments enable investors to invest a fixed amount regularly, leveraging rupee cost averaging.

5. **Cost Averaging over Time**: In both rising and falling markets, RCA helps bring down the average cost per unit compared to lump-sum investments.

6. **Loss Minimization**: RCA reduces the impact of market downturns, as seen in the example where more units were accumulated when prices fell, lessening losses compared to a lump sum approach.

7. **Reduces Timing Risk**: Since investment occurs at regular intervals, it eliminates the risk of making large investments at the wrong time.

8. **Builds Investment Discipline**: Regular, automated investments create a habit of disciplined saving and investing, essential for long-term wealth creation.

9. **Avoids Emotional Investing**: RCA prevents emotional decision-making driven by fear or greed, promoting consistency even in market downturns.

10. **Boosts Long-Term Gains via Compounding**: With consistency and time, RCA supports the power of compounding, helping investors grow wealth steadily over the long term.

Chapter: 12

Retirement vs. Financial Freedom: Understanding the Critical Difference

In personal finance, the terms *retirement* and *financial freedom* are often used interchangeably. While they may seem similar on the surface, they represent fundamentally different life goals with distinct implications for lifestyle, mind-set, and long-term planning. Understanding the difference between these concepts is not just a matter of semantics—it can shape how one designs their financial journey, sets priorities, and makes life-altering decisions.

What is Retirement?

Retirement traditionally refers to the stage in life when an individual stops working, typically after reaching a certain age, often around 60 or 65. This phase is associated with withdrawing from one's career or professional life and relying on savings, pensions, or social security for income. Retirement is generally age-driven and often influenced by societal norms or employment policies.

Retirement has historically been seen as a reward for decades of labor—a time to slow down, relax, and enjoy the fruits of one's hard work. However, it also implies a fixed endpoint to one's working life, whether or not the person is financially ready or personally fulfilled.

What is Financial Freedom?

Financial freedom, on the other hand, refers to having sufficient wealth and income-generating assets to live life on your own terms—regardless of age or traditional timelines. It means no longer being dependent on a paycheck to cover expenses, and having the flexibility to pursue work, travel, passion projects, or philanthropy purely by choice.

Someone who is financially free may choose to work, start a business, or engage in creative pursuits, not out of necessity, but because they are passionate about them. Financial freedom is about choice, control, and peace of mind—not about a specific age or milestone.

Key Differences

Aspect	Retirement	Financial Freedom
Age-related	Typically age-bound	Not age-specific
Work status	No longer working	Work optional

Aspect	Retirement	Financial Freedom
Income source	Passive income or pension	Passive or active by choice
Motivation	End of career	Autonomy and flexibility
Planning focus	Long-term savings	Building wealth and cash flow

Why Understanding the Difference Matters

Recognizing the distinction between retirement and financial freedom has profound implications:

1. **Clarity of Goals:** Without a clear understanding, people may save and plan for retirement without ever exploring the possibility of achieving financial freedom earlier in life.

2. **Better Financial Decisions:** Knowing the difference allows individuals to adopt strategies focused on building assets and cash flow rather than solely saving for the long term.

3. **Lifestyle Design:** Financial freedom empowers individuals to design their lives around what truly matters to them, be it travel, entrepreneurship, or social impact, without waiting for a retirement date.

4. **Psychological Well-being:** Retirement often implies aging and slowing down, while financial freedom feels empowering and energizing.

This shift in mindset can significantly affect motivation and life satisfaction.

Let's explore this difference through three real-life inspired case studies.

Case Study 1: Meera - The Traditional Retiree

Meera, a 62-year-old schoolteacher, spent 35 years in the public education system. She followed a conventional path—saving diligently in her provident fund and pension plan. She looked forward to retirement as a time to finally rest and enjoy her hobbies.

Upon retiring, she found herself financially secure but emotionally unfulfilled. Her pension covered her basic needs, but she missed the sense of purpose and social connection that her job had provided. Although she had reached retirement, she hadn't achieved financial freedom in the broader sense—her lifestyle was limited by a fixed income, and she felt hesitant to explore new ventures due to financial constraints.

Lesson: Retirement without financial freedom can lead to a passive lifestyle, where choices are restricted by a fixed budget and psychological stagnation.

Case Study 2: Ramesh - The Financially Free Entrepreneur

Ramesh, 39, built a successful e-commerce business over a decade. Through smart investing and reinvesting profits into real estate and dividend stocks, he reached a point where his passive income exceeded his monthly expenses.

Although he could "retire" in the conventional sense, Ramesh continued to work on his terms—consulting startups, mentoring young entrepreneurs, and launching a podcast. His work brought him joy and purpose, not because he needed the money, but because he was passionate about innovation and helping others grow.

Lesson: Financial freedom isn't about escaping work; it's about having the freedom to choose meaningful work. Age is irrelevant when you have autonomy.

Case Study 3: Priya and Arjun - The Balanced Planners

Priya and Arjun, a dual-income couple in their early 30s, decided to rethink the idea of retirement. Instead of saving aggressively for a distant retirement, they prioritized financial freedom as a near-term goal. They optimized their expenses, invested in mutual funds, and built multiple income streams through side hustles and rental income.

By the time they turned 45, they had accumulated enough assets to support a simpler, less work-intensive lifestyle. They took a sabbatical, traveled with their kids for a year, and then returned to part-time consulting and volunteering.

Lesson: By focusing on financial freedom rather than traditional retirement, Priya and Arjun experienced the benefits of time, flexibility, and family connection much earlier in life.

Shifting the Narrative

The traditional model of "study hard, work hard, retire at 60" is becoming increasingly outdated. Longer life expectancy, technological changes, and evolving work structures demand a more flexible financial vision.

Here's why the conversation needs to shift from retirement to financial freedom:

- **Life is unpredictable:** Waiting until 60 to live your dreams is risky. Health, family circumstances, or burnout can disrupt that timeline.

- **Purpose doesn't retire:** Many people want to remain active and purposeful beyond retirement age.

- **Freedom is inspiring:** A goal like financial freedom feels more empowering and immediate than a distant retirement.

Action Steps to Aim for Financial Freedom

1. **Define what freedom means to you.** Is it traveling, starting a nonprofit, or spending more time with family?

2. **Track and optimize expenses.** Live below your means and invest the difference.

3. **Create multiple income streams.** Look beyond your salary—consider freelancing, investments, or passive income.

4. **Invest early and consistently.** Compounding works wonders over time.

5. **Educate yourself.** Financial literacy is the foundation of financial freedom.

Final Thoughts

While retirement and financial freedom are both desirable goals, they are not the same—and confusing them can limit one's potential. Retirement is often a default path dictated by external factors, while financial freedom is a conscious pursuit fuelled by clarity, discipline, and purpose.

By shifting focus from "when can I stop working?" to "how can I live life on my own terms?" we open doors to a more empowered, intentional, and fulfilling life.

Here's a 10-point summary of the content "Retirement vs. Financial Freedom: Understanding the Critical Difference":

1. **Conceptual Difference**: *Retirement* is traditionally age-based and signals the end of a career, while *financial freedom* means having enough resources to live on your own terms, regardless of age.

2. **Work Status**: Retirement implies not working at all, whereas financial freedom means work becomes optional—not necessary for survival, but a choice.

3. **Source of Income**: Retirees usually rely on pensions or savings; financially free individuals depend on passive income or active income by choice.

4. **Mindset and Motivation**: Retirement often symbolizes slowing down, while financial freedom reflects autonomy, energy, and the pursuit of passion or purpose.

5. **Planning Focus**: Retirement planning emphasizes long-term savings, whereas financial freedom focuses on building wealth, cash flow, and multiple income streams.

6. **Real-Life Impacts**: Case studies show that retirement can lead to stagnation (e.g., Meera),

while financial freedom enables dynamic, fulfilling lives (e.g., Ramesh, Priya & Arjun).

7. **Psychological Implications**: Financial freedom tends to boost self-worth and satisfaction, while traditional retirement may lead to emotional voids or limited lifestyle choices.

8. **Lifestyle Design**: Financial freedom allows people to design flexible lives that include travel, entrepreneurship, and family time—well before the typical retirement age.

9. **Changing Times**: The old "work until 60" model is outdated. With longer lifespans and modern work options, financial freedom offers a more adaptive and resilient path.

10. **Actionable Steps**: Define your version of freedom, track expenses, build income streams, invest early, and educate yourself—these are key to achieving financial freedom.

Chapter: 13

Understanding Investor Risk Profiles: Types, Importance, and the Process of Risk Profiling

When it comes to investing, one of the most fundamental steps is understanding an investor's **risk profile**. Every investor has a different tolerance for risk, shaped by their financial goals, time horizon, income, age, personality, and past experiences. Without a clear understanding of an investor's risk profile, even the most technically sound investment strategy may fail to deliver satisfaction or appropriate results.

In this chapter, we'll explore:

- What is a risk profile?

- Different types of investor risk profiles

- How to conduct risk profiling

- Mistakes to avoid in risk profiling

What is an Investor Risk Profile?

An **investor risk profile** is a comprehensive assessment that determines an individual's willingness and ability to take financial risk. It serves as a cornerstone for building a customized investment strategy. Risk profiling doesn't only consider the desire to take risk (risk appetite) but also the capacity to bear risk (risk tolerance), and the investor's financial situation (risk requirement).

A properly conducted risk profile helps in selecting suitable investment products and asset allocations, aligning with the investor's comfort zone and objectives. Misjudging this profile can lead to portfolio mismatch, investment anxiety, or worse, substantial financial losses.

Types of Investor Risk Profiles

Investor risk profiles can be broadly categorized into the following types:

1. Conservative

A conservative investor prioritizes capital preservation over high returns. They are averse to market volatility and prefer investments with stable and predictable income such as fixed deposits, bonds, or debt mutual funds.

Key Characteristics:

- Low risk tolerance
- Prefers safety over growth

- Long investment horizon, but little appetite for market fluctuations

- Often retired individuals or those close to retirement

2. Moderately Conservative

These investors are slightly more open to market-linked instruments, but still lean toward safer options. A small portion of the portfolio may be allocated to equities, but the bulk remains in fixed-income assets.

Key Characteristics:

- Low to moderate risk tolerance

- Willing to accept minimal losses for slightly better returns

- Usually middle-aged investors building wealth slowly

3. Moderate

A balanced approach defines this profile. These investors seek a mix of stability and growth, often opting for a 50-50 or 60-40 split between equities and debt.

Key Characteristics:

- Balanced risk appetite

- Comfortable with moderate volatility

- Goal-oriented, with a medium to long-term outlook

4. Moderately Aggressive

This type leans more toward growth and is willing to take calculated risks. They accept higher volatility for potentially better long-term gains.

Key Characteristics:

- Higher risk tolerance

- Greater exposure to equities

- Typically younger investors with long-term financial goals like retirement or wealth accumulation

5. Aggressive

Aggressive investors thrive on market opportunities and are not rattled by volatility. They often aim for the highest possible returns, even if it means facing significant short-term losses.

Key Characteristics:

- High risk tolerance

- Primarily invest in equities, alternative investments, or even startups

- Typically young, financially secure, and experienced in investing

Why Is Risk Profiling Important?

Risk profiling is not just a regulatory checkbox for financial advisors—it's crucial for ethical and effective investment planning. Here's why:

- **Prevents Mis-selling:** Accurate profiling ensures that advisors recommend suitable products that match the investor's comfort and capacity.

- **Improves Investor Confidence:** When investors understand and agree with the investment strategy, they're more likely to stay invested during volatile periods.

- **Facilitates Goal Alignment:** It helps align investment decisions with life goals and financial circumstances.

- **Reduces Emotional Investing:** Proper profiling helps mitigate panic during downturns or euphoria during booms.

How to Conduct Risk Profiling

Risk profiling involves a mix of qualitative and quantitative methods. Financial advisors, wealth managers, or even digital investment platforms usually conduct this exercise at the beginning of the investment journey.

Here's how the process typically unfolds:

1. Use of Risk Assessment Questionnaires

These are structured forms that gather insights about:

- Age and financial background

- Income and expenses

- Investment experience

- Time horizon for goals

- Attitude toward market fluctuations

- Reaction to hypothetical gains and losses

The answers are usually scored, with cumulative results indicating the risk category the investor fits into.

2. Understanding Financial Capacity

This evaluates the **ability** to take risk, which includes:

- Regular income

- Net worth

- Existing debt

- Number of dependents

- Emergency fund availability

An investor may be willing to take high risks but might lack the financial cushion to do so—leading to an adjustment in the profile.

3. Analyzing Investment Objectives

Are they saving for a house in 5 years or retirement in 25 years? The nature and timeframe of goals influence what kind of risk is acceptable.

For example:

- Short-term goals usually require low-risk instruments.

- Long-term goals can accommodate market volatility for higher returns.

4. Behavioural Assessment

This includes a subjective evaluation of how an investor behaves under stress. It's often based on prior investing experiences and reactions during market downturns. While difficult to quantify, behavioural clues are crucial for understanding real risk tolerance.

Common Mistakes to Avoid in Risk Profiling

- **Ignoring behavioural cues:** Sometimes the numbers indicate high tolerance, but investor behaviour says otherwise.

- **One-size-fits-all questionnaires:** Not tailoring the questionnaire to the investor's background can lead to misleading results.

- **Neglecting communication:** Failing to explain risk concepts to the investor may result in poor understanding and misguided choices.

- **Static profiling:** Investors evolve, and their risk profiles must adapt accordingly.

Final Thoughts

Risk profiling is not just a compliance requirement—it's the foundation for a well-tailored investment journey. Identifying the correct risk profile empowers investors to make informed decisions, helps advisors offer suitable products, and ultimately contributes to long-term wealth creation.

Whether you're a DIY investor or working with a financial planner, take risk profiling seriously. Reflect on your goals, understand your own behaviour toward risk, and make sure your investments mirror your financial identity.

After all, investing isn't about chasing the highest returns—it's about reaching your goals with peace of mind

Here's a 10-point summary of the content on *Understanding Investor Risk Profiles: Types, Importance, and the Process of Risk Profiling:*

1. **Definition of Risk Profile**: An investor's risk profile evaluates their willingness and ability to take financial risks, combining risk appetite, tolerance, and requirement to guide investment strategy.

2. **Purpose**: A clear risk profile ensures investment choices align with personal financial goals, reducing stress and preventing mismatched portfolios.

3. **Types of Risk Profiles**: Investors are categorized into five broad profiles—Conservative, Moderately Conservative, Moderate, Moderately Aggressive, and Aggressive—based on their comfort with risk and return expectations.

4. **Conservative Investors**: Prefer capital safety over returns; they avoid volatility and stick to stable instruments like bonds or fixed deposits.

5. **Aggressive Investors**: Embrace volatility for high returns, often investing heavily in equities and alternative assets; usually young and financially secure.

6. **Importance of Risk Profiling**: It prevents mis-selling, builds investor confidence, aligns investments with life goals, and reduces emotional decision-making.

7. **Risk Profiling Process**: Involves questionnaires, financial capacity evaluation, goal analysis, and behavioural assessments to understand both objective and subjective risk factors.

8. **Questionnaires and Scoring**: Standard tools used to gather and score data on investor background, financial status, and responses to hypothetical scenarios.

9. **Common Mistakes**: Includes ignoring behaviour cues, using generic tools, poor communication, and treating the risk profile as static despite changing life circumstances.

10. **Conclusion**: Risk profiling is the foundation of smart investing—investors should regularly revisit their profile and ensure their strategy matches their evolving goals and financial identity.

Chapter: 14

Do-It-Yourself vs. Financial Advisor: Making the Right Choice for Your Investments

One of the most frequently debated topics in the world of investing is whether to manage your money on your own—commonly known as **Do-It-Yourself (DIY) investing**—or to engage the services of a **financial advisor**. With the internet offering a vast pool of free resources, tutorials, tools, and data, the temptation to take control of your own financial journey is understandable. But is it the best route for everyone?

The truth is, **there is no one-size-fits-all answer**. Both options have their advantages and drawbacks. Let's explore the key considerations that can help you determine the most suitable path for your financial goals.

Understanding the Complexity of Investing

Investing is far more than just picking a stock or buying a mutual fund. It involves multiple layers of decisions that require both technical knowledge and strategic thinking. Some of the core aspects include:

1. Choosing the right asset classes (equity, debt, real estate, etc.)

2. Timing your investments—when to enter and exit

3. Structuring your portfolio for optimal performance

4. Assessing and balancing risk and return

5. Ensuring proper diversification

6. Staying updated on tax regulations

7. Aligning investments with short-term and long-term financial goals

These tasks aren't static—they evolve as markets, economic conditions, and personal circumstances change. Therefore, the real question becomes: **Do you have the time and the expertise to manage this process on your own?**

The Two Big Questions to Ask Yourself

Before deciding between DIY investing and hiring a financial advisor, ask yourself:

1. **Can I devote enough time to monitor, manage, and adjust my investments regularly?**

2. Do I possess the necessary knowledge and understanding to make sound investment decisions?

These two parameters—**time** and **knowledge**—are crucial. If your answer to either of them is **"no,"** then seeking professional help is not only wise but potentially more rewarding in the long run.

The Information & Analytical Edge

We live in an era where information is abundant and often free. Numerous websites and platforms offer data on direct equities, mutual funds, real estate, commodities, and more. Analytical tools are available to help dissect past performance, compare funds, and even assess risk.

However, **access to information doesn't automatically translate into insight**. Many retail investors struggle with interpreting data correctly or applying it effectively to their own unique financial circumstances.

A financial advisor bridges this gap by:

- Bringing deep, real-world experience

- Filtering out the noise and focusing on relevant, actionable information

- Tailoring investment strategies to your financial objectives, time horizon, and risk appetite

They are not just information providers; they're **decision facilitators**.

The Behavioral Advantage: Managing Emotions in Investing

Investing is not purely logical. It's deeply emotional. Fear and greed—the two dominant emotions in investing—can cloud judgment and lead to impulsive decisions. This is where a financial advisor can make a significant difference.

A competent advisor serves as a **behavioral coach**, helping you stay focused and rational, especially in volatile markets. Here's how:

- Preventing emotionally-driven decisions (like panic selling or chasing hype)

- Encouraging a long-term mindset

- Helping you stick to your financial plan through market cycles

- Acting as a gatekeeper to avoid impulsive or misaligned investments

Think of a financial advisor as a **doctor for your financial health**—offering preventive care, providing timely interventions, and performing portfolio "surgery" when needed. Just as self-medication can lead to harmful outcomes, unmanaged investments can lead to poor financial health.

Investing is a Journey, Not a One-Time Event

Another common misconception is that investing is a one-off activity. In reality, it's a **continuous process** that demands discipline, consistency, and adaptability.

You may score a few short-term wins with some DIY strategies or lucky picks. But building **long-term, sustainable, and generational wealth** requires a guided approach. Investment needs also differ greatly from person to person—your financial plan must reflect your specific life stage, goals, responsibilities, and risk tolerance.

There's no universal solution. What works for one individual or family may not work for another. A financial advisor helps personalize your strategy and adjusts it as your life and the economic landscape evolve.

Busting the Myth: "Advisors Are Too Expensive"

One of the most persistent myths in investing is that hiring a financial advisor eats into your returns due to their fees or commissions. While it's true that advisors charge for their services, this cost should be viewed through the lens of **value, not just expense**.

Here's what a good financial advisor actually does for you:

- Educates you on investment options tailored to your needs

- Conducts in-depth risk assessments and recommends suitable asset classes

- Constructs and manages a well-diversified, goal-aligned portfolio

- Rebalances your investments as needed based on market trends and personal goals

- Serves as a trusted partner who safeguards your money from impulsive or misinformed decisions

In short, they **add value that often outweighs the cost**. They help you avoid costly mistakes, enhance long-term performance, and provide peace of mind—allowing you to focus on your life while your money works for you.

There's no such thing as a free lunch in life—or in investing. The small fee paid to an advisor is often the cost of **avoiding larger losses** that could result from inexperience, emotional investing, or neglect.

Final Thoughts: Choosing What's Right for You

Ultimately, the decision between DIY investing and hiring a financial advisor comes down to your personal preferences, lifestyle, and financial literacy. If you're someone who enjoys learning about markets, has the time to stay updated, and can maintain emotional discipline—you might thrive as a DIY investor.

But if you're pressed for time, overwhelmed by financial jargon, or prone to emotional decision-making, working with a financial advisor might be the smartest investment you make.

Whether you do it yourself or work with a professional, the key is to **stay engaged, stay informed, and stay committed** to your financial goals. After all, investing isn't just about money—it's about building the life you want to live.

Here's a 10-point summary of the article "Do-It-Yourself vs. Financial Advisor: Making the Right Choice for Your Investments":

1. **DIY vs. Advisor Debate:** With abundant online resources, DIY investing is appealing, but it's not suitable for everyone—both approaches have pros and cons depending on the individual.

2. **Investing Is Complex**: Successful investing requires knowledge in asset allocation, timing, risk management, diversification, tax laws, and goal alignment—it's far from simple.

3. **Time and Knowledge Are Key**: Before choosing a path, assess if you have the time and expertise to consistently manage your investments effectively.

4. **Access Doesn't Equal Insight**: While free data and tools are widely available, many investors

struggle to interpret and apply them meaningfully to their personal situations.

5. **Role of a Financial Advisor**: Advisors offer tailored strategies, cut through information overload, and provide expert guidance aligned with your goals and risk tolerance.

6. **Emotional Discipline**: Investing is emotional—advisors act as behavioral coaches to help clients avoid panic-selling or impulsive decisions during market fluctuations.

7. **Investing Is a Lifelong Journey**: It's an ongoing process requiring adaptation and discipline—not a one-time action. Personalized planning is key to long-term success.

8. **Personalization Matters**: Financial strategies must be customized to individual life stages, responsibilities, and financial aspirations—there's no universal solution.

9. **Cost vs. Value Myth**: While advisors charge fees, their value often exceeds the cost through risk mitigation, performance enhancement, and helping avoid costly mistakes.

10. **Make the Right Choice for You**: Your decision should reflect your lifestyle, interest in finance, time availability, and emotional discipline. Either way, staying engaged and committed is essential.

Chapter: 15

Life Insurance: An Investment Viewpoint

A financial goal plan would most commonly consist of following goals:

a) Buying a New House

b) Buying a New Car

c) Investing for Child's Education

d) Investing for Child's Wedding

e) Investing for Retirement Corpus

The bread winner of a family plans for saving and investing as per the requirement of these goals once he/she starts earning. Among this, while purchasing a house property or a car, he/she may borrow money over & above the amount of down payment. Now, in this journey, what if there is an untimely demise of the bread winner of a family i.e. before completion of all these goals he/she is no more. There's an emotional loss as well as financial loss to the family. That's the reason why one needs a life insurance.

Protecting the fulfilment of required goals for financial dependents against the risk of untimely demise of a bread winner is the most commonly understood aspect of life insurance.

BUT… This is not it!!

There's a broader perspective when you think of planning for a life cover. Life insurance is not just your safety net. It is a tool for your legacy. It is an investment towards protecting your legacy. The common things for which this tool can be used for are:

1. **Asset Equalization:**

    Suppose you have three kids. Two are daughters and one is a son. Let's say son is not into the business but both daughter are into it. But you still want to leave a large legacy for your son. In that case, you can put a large policy for your son to have it and you are able to use this tool as equalizing your asset transfer.

2. **Asset Preservation:**

    Progressively, in life you will accumulate and build wealth & assets. These assets would be directly or indirectly exposed to market risk. When you have built and accumulated these assets and all are subject to market risk; however you can actually hedge them by wrapping them with a life insurance policy on place.

Consequently, this becomes an investment to preserve your assets.

3. Asset Transfer:

Asset transfer comes with a lot of procedural & compliance exercise. When you are transferring the asset and trying to mitigate taxes as well as preventing from many other complicated compliance requirements, you can again use life insurance proceeds as a tool for liquidity and create more assets for your family.

These three things and many more things are what life insurance is used for. That's why I call life insurance is a perfect tool to create wealth. One of the smart move in financial planning is investing in life insurance as tool to build legacy for your family as well as business especially now when there is an option to buy whole life cover as well.

You, Your Business & Your Legacy

Asset equalization in business through life insurance is also helpful **to mitigate Key Man Risk**. As a business owner, you are building & managing an organization where you have also employed people to work for your business goals. You along with these employees are primarily dependent on the organization for primary-active source of income. Hence you are considered a Key Personnel of your business. Sometimes your absence for a day or two might have put the organizational affairs on hold. So, imagine the pain the business may go through if you are absent permanently.

The first thing your organization will need is a personnel who is your equivalent; in terms of talent, responsibility & accountability for continuity of business. Remember, this does not happen free of cost. Organization will have to hire and designate a Key Personnel at your position which comes with a cost. Until the appointment of a new key person, there might be an opportunity cost to the organization due to lack of appropriate decision making. Do you want to pay this cost out of organization's net worth or your personal savings in your absence? **Clearly No.**

That's where, Keyman Life Insurance becomes a tool for business continuity planning and legacy of an organization & its stakeholders. Tax benefits of related expenditure as well as the tax efficient receipts of maturity amount will be an added advantage to the organization. These features makes keyman life insurance a worthy investment.

A broader business Perspective

An adequate life insurance on place is also treated as a separate business vertical. Being a person who is running the business, the assets, investments, liabilities and the business itself are all exposed to market risks.

Thus many large houses and families treat their life insurance protection as a separate business vertical. This means you spend a little operating cost to ensure a lumpsum benefit out of a business in case of a permanent loss of keyman. Thus this becomes a part of core wealth creation strategy for an entity. Consequently, this will add to the surplus on the balance sheet of business which eventually can be very fruitful.

The Legacy Story

We treat life insurance merely as a safety tool. However as you can clearly see, it is way beyond just a safety net. General tendency is that we underestimate the wealth creation aspect of life insurance and that's where we miss the opportunity to capitalize on creating multi-generational wealth.

The strategy of having a whole life insurance allows you to use assets efficiently, maintain control of assets and meet desired distributions at the time of wealth transfer.

By this, you are providing financial protection, improving financial well-being, giving a potential source of funding requirements and writing a great legacy story.

Here's a 10-point summary of the content titled "Life Insurance: An Investment Viewpoint":

1. **Financial Goals & Risks**: Individuals typically plan for major life goals like buying a house, a car, and investing for children's education, marriage, and retirement. The untimely death of the family's breadwinner can derail these goals, highlighting the need for life insurance.

2. **Primary Purpose of Life Insurance**: It acts as a safety net to protect the financial future of dependents in case of the policyholder's untimely demise.

3. **Beyond Protection – Legacy Planning**: Life insurance is also a powerful tool for legacy planning and wealth creation, not just risk coverage.

4. **Asset Equalization**: Life insurance can help balance inheritance among heirs, especially when business or asset involvement varies among children.

5. **Asset Preservation**: Insurance can act as a hedge against market risks affecting accumulated wealth, thus preserving the value of assets.

6. **Asset Transfer & Liquidity**: Insurance helps simplify asset transfer, provide liquidity, and reduce tax and compliance burdens during inheritance.

7. **Business Continuity – Keyman Insurance**: For business owners, life insurance can cover the cost of replacing key personnel, ensuring business continuity after the owner's death.

8. **Tax & Financial Advantages for Business**: Keyman insurance offers tax benefits and acts as a financial cushion, reducing operational disruptions and preserving business value.

9. **Life Insurance as a Business Strategy**: Large business families treat life insurance as a separate business vertical—a strategic investment for long-term wealth creation and risk mitigation.

10. **Multi-Generational Wealth & Control**: Whole life insurance enables better control over asset usage and distribution, creating sustainable, multi-generational wealth and a strong financial legacy.

Chapter: 16

Embracing Financial Change: The Importance of Regular Portfolio Reviews

One of the few constants in life is change. This universal truth holds especially true in personal finance. Whether it's a shift in your income, a change in life stage, or evolving financial goals, change is inevitable—and your investment strategy must evolve alongside it. A static approach to money management can result in missed opportunities, unaddressed risks, and a failure to meet important life goals. That's why reviewing and adjusting your financial portfolio regularly is not just recommended—it's essential.

Why Financial Strategies Must Evolve

When you begin your investment journey, your financial decisions are shaped by a combination of factors unique to your personal circumstances:

- Age and stage of life

- Income and expenses

- Short- and long-term financial goals

- Standard and quality of living

- Risk tolerance

- Financial dependents

- Financial literacy and awareness

Each of these elements is dynamic. A promotion, a new family member, a career break, or even a global economic downturn can shift the financial equation. Consequently, your financial plan should never be carved in stone. Instead, it should act as a living document—flexible and responsive.

Annual Reviews: A Financial Health Check-up

Just like you go for an annual health check-up to prevent illnesses and detect issues early, your financial portfolio requires similar attention. An annual review ensures that your investments are aligned with your evolving needs and that you're not exposed to risks you can't afford—or missing opportunities for growth.

Let's explore how life's changing nature necessitates regular financial check-ins.

Real-Life Examples: Financial Planning in Motion

Case 1: Mr. Aalok's Entrepreneurial Journey

Aalok started his business at 27, when he was unmarried and financially independent. Understanding the need for protection, he immediately bought a term insurance plan with a ₹1 crore cover. Over the next three years, his business flourished, and his income tripled. At 31, he got married, which introduced new financial dependencies and goals.

Financial Shifts:

- Significant increase in income

- Change in life stage and dependents

Portfolio Review Recommendation:

Aalok needs to reassess the adequacy of his life cover. A ₹1 crore insurance policy may have been sufficient when he was single with modest income, but it's likely inadequate now that his financial responsibilities have increased. He should also revisit his savings strategy to accommodate new goals such as home ownership, children's education, and wealth preservation.

Case 2: Ms. Meera's Retirement Transition

Meera worked in the corporate world for 30 years. Starting at 25, she consistently invested via monthly SIPs in equity mutual funds, building a robust retirement corpus of ₹12 crores by the age of 55. Now retired, her sole income is a monthly pension.

Financial Shifts:

- Transition from active earner to retiree

- No salary; pension becomes primary income source

Portfolio Review Recommendation:

With retirement, Meera's priorities have shifted from aggressive wealth accumulation to income stability and capital preservation. A portfolio that was 100% equity-based during her earning years may now be too volatile. She should consider reallocating a portion of her corpus into more stable instruments like debt funds, fixed income products, or annuities to ensure reliable cash flow and reduce exposure to market volatility.

These examples illustrate how personal finance is not a one-size-fits-all concept. Every individual's financial journey is unique, and periodic reviews are essential to ensure continued alignment with changing realities.

Framework for a Comprehensive Portfolio Review

Conducting a portfolio review involves evaluating multiple facets of your financial life. Here's a structured framework to guide your process:

1. Insurance: Protection First

Life and Personal Accident Insurance

- Is your term insurance coverage sufficient for your current income and family needs?

- Do your insurance policies reflect your current liabilities and dependents?

Health Insurance

- Is your health coverage adequate considering inflation in medical costs?

- Are the features of your policy—like co-pay clauses, network hospitals, and exclusions—still relevant?

2. Financial Goals: Tracking the Destination

- Have you documented your short- and long-term financial goals?

- Are your investments tagged to specific goals?

- Do you have a clear view of which goals are on track and which ones show a surplus or deficit?

3. Investments: Balancing Growth and Stability

- Is your current asset allocation aligned with your risk appetite and time horizon?

- Are any of your investments underperforming consistently? If yes, do you understand why?

- Are your investments well diversified, or are you overexposed to a particular sector or asset class?

4. Assets and Liabilities: Understanding the Net Worth Equation

- Have you updated records for all your assets—real estate, equity, debt instruments, gold, etc.?

- Are your EMIs manageable within your current cash flows?

- Can you prepay any high-interest debt to reduce liabilities?

- Are you prioritizing debt repayment effectively (e.g., closing high-interest loans first)?

Risks of Neglecting Portfolio Reviews

Skipping your annual financial check-up might seem harmless in the short term, but it can have long-lasting negative effects on your financial well-being. Here are the major pitfalls:

1. **Excessive Churning**

   While it may seem proactive to constantly switch funds or investments, excessive churning can lead to higher transaction costs, tax implications, and missed compounding opportunities. It's essential to differentiate between proactive adjustments and impulsive reactions to market noise.

2. **Being Too Passive**

   On the flip side, neglecting your portfolio can be equally dangerous. Market fluctuations can alter your asset allocation and risk profile. Without a timely review, you may continue holding underperforming or high-risk investments that no longer serve your objectives.

3. Scattered and Over-Diversified Portfolio

Many investors believe that more is better. But owning too many mutual funds, stocks, or insurance policies can lead to a lack of focus, duplication of investments, and difficulty in performance tracking. Studies suggest that over-diversification may dilute returns and complicate portfolio management.

Steps to Conduct an Effective Portfolio Review

A structured approach ensures that your review yields actionable insights:

Step 1: Evaluate Current Holdings

Make a list of all your investments—mutual funds, stocks, FDs, insurance policies, real estate, etc. Assess each holding's performance, risk profile, and contribution to your financial goals.

Step 2: Review Asset Allocation

Check if your current allocation between equity, debt, real estate, gold, and other instruments aligns with your target mix. Rebalance if needed to maintain the desired level of risk and return.

Step 3: Reassess Risk Tolerance

Your risk appetite may change over time due to age, income, health, or market conditions. Ensure that your investment strategy reflects your current comfort level with risk.

Step 4: Rebalance the Portfolio

Based on your findings, reallocate your investments to regain your ideal asset allocation. This could involve shifting funds from equity to debt, or vice versa, depending on your stage of life and market outlook.

Step 5: Set the Next Review Date

Put your review schedule on autopilot. Set calendar reminders for bi-annual or annual reviews. Consider syncing your review with major life events (e.g., job change, marriage, childbirth, or retirement).

Emotional Discipline: The Key to Effective Reviews

One often-overlooked aspect of financial reviews is emotional control. Panic selling during market downturns or FOMO-driven investing during bull markets can derail your financial plan. During your review, rely on logic and long-term strategy rather than emotion or market hype. If needed, consult a financial advisor to get a neutral, expert opinion.

Conclusion: A Dynamic Approach to Personal Finance

Personal finance is not a "set it and forget it" game. It's a lifelong journey that requires continuous attention and adaptability. As your life changes, so too should your financial strategies. Regular reviews not only safeguard your wealth but also empower you to make informed, timely decisions that align with your evolving goals.

In the end, successful financial planning isn't about predicting the future—it's about preparing for it. With a disciplined review process in place, you'll be better equipped to adapt to change, protect what you've built, and continue growing toward your dreams.

Here's a 10-point summary for *"Embracing Financial Change: The Importance of Regular Portfolio Reviews"*

1. Change Is the Only Constant—Even in Finance

Life is in a constant state of flux—new jobs, growing families, lifestyle upgrades, economic shifts. Personal finance is no exception. What worked for you financially a few years ago may no longer be effective today. That's why your investment strategy should evolve as your circumstances change. A static financial plan can lead to missed opportunities, increased risks, or misalignment with life goals.

2. Financial Strategies Must Evolve with You

Your investment decisions are influenced by dynamic factors like age, income, family responsibilities, risk appetite, and financial literacy. A 25-year-old single professional will have a vastly different financial profile compared to a 50-year-old nearing retirement. Since these variables aren't fixed, your portfolio shouldn't be either. It should be treated as a living, breathing plan—adaptable and responsive to the shifts in your life.

3. Annual Portfolio Reviews: Your Financial Health Check-Up

Just as an annual medical check-up helps detect health issues early, an annual financial review can reveal inefficiencies in your portfolio and protect against potential pitfalls. These reviews ensure that your investments continue to align with your goals, risk tolerance, and income changes. Regular reviews are proactive measures that help keep your financial trajectory on track.

4. Real-Life Lessons: The Need for Timely Adjustments

Through examples like Mr. Aalok, a young entrepreneur whose responsibilities and income changed dramatically within a few years, and Ms. Meera, a retiree shifting from accumulation to preservation, the article highlights the necessity of reviewing insurance cover, asset allocation, and risk exposure based on current life stages. These stories underscore that financial planning is highly individual and time-sensitive.

5. A Structured Framework for Portfolio Reviews

Effective reviews aren't just about glancing at account balances—they require a structured approach:

- **Insurance**: Is your life and health cover still relevant to your needs and liabilities?

- **Financial Goals**: Are your investments aligned with specific goals, and are those goals still realistic?

- **Investments**: Are your assets balanced between growth and stability? Any underperforming ones?

- **Net Worth**: Have you reviewed your assets and liabilities? Are your EMIs sustainable? Can any high-interest debt be cleared early?

This comprehensive view helps ensure you're managing both growth and risk efficiently.

6. The Hidden Dangers of Skipping Reviews

Neglecting portfolio reviews can silently erode your financial wellbeing. Key risks include:

- **Excessive churning**: Frequently switching investments without strategy can lead to high costs and loss of compounding benefits.

- **Being too passive**: Ignoring your portfolio might result in holding outdated or risky investments.

- **Over-diversification**: Owning too many funds or policies may seem smart but can dilute returns and complicate tracking.

Reviews help you find the sweet spot between action and inaction.

7. Five Clear Steps for an Effective Portfolio Review

To extract meaningful outcomes from your review, follow a step-by-step process:

1. **List current holdings**: Know what you own and why.

2. **Check asset allocation**: Is your equity-debt balance appropriate for your age and goals?

3. **Reassess risk tolerance**: Have your emotional and financial capacity for risk changed?

4. **Rebalance your portfolio**: Adjust to restore your ideal mix.

5. **Schedule the next review**: Treat this like a recurring calendar event tied to milestones or life changes.

This structure ensures your financial plan remains dynamic and focused.

8. Emotional Discipline: The Unsung Hero of Smart Investing

Emotions often sabotage even the most well-planned investment strategies. Panic during market drops or greed during bull runs can lead to poor decisions. During your reviews, it's crucial to remain calm, rational, and long-term focused. Avoid knee-jerk reactions and resist the urge to "time" the market. When in doubt, consult a financial advisor to bring objectivity and professional insight to the table.

9. Portfolio Reviews as a Long-Term Wealth Strategy

Regular portfolio reviews are not just for damage control—they're powerful tools for wealth creation. They help you capitalize on evolving market opportunities, eliminate inefficiencies, and stay ahead of financial risks. Whether you're a seasoned investor or just starting out, the act of reviewing keeps your strategy aligned with real-life progress.

Moreover, reviews help refine your goals. You might realize that you're ahead on retirement savings and can now focus more on travel or philanthropy. Or maybe your child's education fund needs beefing up. Without regular reviews, these nuances remain hidden.

10. Conclusion: Stay Prepared, Stay Empowered

Ultimately, personal finance is about preparation, not prediction. You can't control market crashes, job changes, or health emergencies—but you *can* control how well you're prepared for them. Regular portfolio reviews ensure that your financial plan is always in tune with your current reality and future aspirations.

By embracing change, reassessing your strategy periodically, and maintaining emotional discipline, you empower yourself to not just manage money—but master it. In a world of uncertainty, that's your greatest financial strength.